WHAT OTHERS ARE SAYING ABOUT

DIVING
INTO THE DEEP

I bought your book and couldn't stop reading ...What a great life for The Lord. There is no telling how many souls have been saved through your many ministries, and how many you are still touching every day. Your book was very uplifting. Keep telling your stories and may God bless you.
C Anthony

I bought your book and couldn't put it down. **It has touched me as much as any Christian book I have read** *since I have been preaching these 48 years. I trust that the Lord gives you a few more years so others can hear it. By God's grace I'm going to dive deeper.*
N Hendrigsman

Wish I could give this 10 stars! *What an amazing book! Bought this after meeting Lowell Lytle (aka Capt. Smith) at the Titanic Museum in Pigeon Forge. Our world would be so different if everyone had the amazing faith & complete trust in the Lord that this man has!* **I highly recommend this book to all young people starting out in life!** *Would be an absolutely perfect graduation gift! Such amazing lessons about how to allow God to lead your decision making, & stepping out in complete & absolute trust that he will provide!*
Amazon Reviews

Thank you for your story ...not only has it brought me closer to my son but also to God, which I am very grateful for. **You are a true inspiration, and your book will be going into our church libary.**
K Reno

...such an inspiring journey of faith. **I felt like I was right there with you on your adventures.** *The book is so well-written, and you've led such an incredible life. I so admire your personal relationship with God and hope my own will continue to grow and hope to find the Faith Rest at all times in life.*
L Myers

Continued

*I would just like to say this is **one of the best books I ever read.** God has truly blessed you. Thank you,*
G Masson

*His writing is just as alluring as his appearance as Captain Smith when he engages his audience in wonderful and true stories of Titanic passengers. **A great book with very intriguing insights into a man's walk with God.** The author takes us on many adventures in his life history ...hundreds of fascinating readings in this great book. Thank you for sharing with us all God's faithfulness to you and for reminding me of the great God that I serve.*
S Miller

*... **an amazing book that I plan on sharing with my friends.** It has taught me that I need to trust God for all things big and small. God Bless you Lowell!*
J Lawson

I'm encouraged by your recounting of His faithfulness in your life. At 58, I too am learning to rest more and more in what He has planned for me, regardless of what it brings. Living by faith in the one true God is an adventure that never stops.
M Parker

You have encouraged me to be more diligent in my walk and see how God can use me to spread the message of His Gospel about His Son Jesus. Thank you so much for being an inspiration to so many...
S. E. Anson

*I wanted to tell you how much I loved your book! From the time I opened it and started reading, **I could not put it down until I had read every single page!** You are 100% right. He has a plan and purpose for all of us! I know beyond a shadow of a doubt that you are walking in His perfect will! May He keep you and bless you all the days of your life!*
D Sparks

PAT BOONE
■ ENTERPRISES

Dear Lowell:

Your book is terrific! You not only led a fascinating life–you know how to write about it in a fascinating way.

I've laughed many times, applauded you many times, and I particularly love your picture on 209. I have a similar sense of humor!

Congratulations - hope our "paths cross again."

God bless you,

Pat

DIVING
INTO THE DEEP

DIVING
INTO THE DEEP

A GRIPPING TRUE STORY OF
ADVENTURE, RISK, AND SPIRITUAL QUEST

LOWELL LYTLE

WITH LESLIE TURNER

Encourage Publishing
New Albany, Indiana

Library of Congress Control Number: 2017933578

Cataloguing data:
Lowell Lytle, Leslie Turner
Diving into the Deep: A Gripping True Story of Adventure,
Risk, and Spiritual Quest

ISBN 97809962067-5-4 (paperback ed.)
ISBN 97809962067-4-7 (hardback ed.)
ISBN 97809962067-3-0 (audiobook ed.)
ISBN 97809962067-6-1 (Limited Collector's ed.)

1. Oral communication-Religious aspects-Christianity.
2. Christian biography   3. Persuasion (Psychology)

Dewey Decimal Classification: 248.9: Christian practice and
observance, Christian life

All scripture quotations are from the Holy Bible, King James Version and
New International Version.

Front Cover art by Roger Bansemer, www.bansemer.com
Overall Cover Design by Jacquelyn Thayer, Nashville, Tennessee
727-577-2963

Published by:

ENCOURAGE
P U B L I S H I N G

Encourage Publishing, LLC
New Albany, Indiana 47150
www.encouragebooks.com

Printed in the United States
For Worldwide Distribution

DEDICATION

I dedicate this book to the memory of my beloved wife, Barbara.

SPECIAL THANKS

Lowell Lytle with Leslie Turner at Kojak's in Tampa, Florida

The stories you are about to read are all true. However, I have so many stories that it would be difficult for one book to contain them all. I'm an entertainer, not a professional writer, so I needed someone who had writing ability, someone who would know which stories to put in and which ones to leave out. I needed someone who would know how to divide them all into chapters and arrange them to make it an interesting read. Before I had completely finished the book, God sent that person my way—another miracle on its own. Her name is Leslie Turner, and she's not just an editor; she's an extremely talented writer who can fill in all the gaps to make the stories flow. She has put in many hours on this project, for which I am extremely grateful. She is a perfect example of what love and giving is all about. Thank you, Leslie.

I've told some of my stories over the past twenty years to many people, but one in particular was a friend of mine who kept telling me that I needed to write a book about them. His name is Scott Brennis. Had Scott not been so persistent, this book would probably have never been written. My hat's off to you, Scott. You made it happen.

A few of my closest friends and many family members spent considerable time and effort critiquing chapters, helping gather photographs, and providing encouragement and moral support. Thanks to all of you. Special thanks to David and Vessela Lytle, Joe Lathrop, Gary and Connie Kolosey, Steve Bishop, Lynella Wiley, Jackie Thayer, Debbie Lytle, and Laura and Cody Smith.

Special thanks as well to Mary Kellogg, Mike Harris, Brenda Wood, Paul Turner, Stan Arthur, Roger Bansemer, and Joe Brown for your generous time, contributions and input. Also, thank you to McDougal and Associates, who helped us with our first journey into the publishing world.

Since its original publication, "Diving into the Deep" has been released in both hardback and paperback, as an audiobook and an e-book as well as being re-released in print with more photos, a few minor corrections, and a wonderful new "bonus" story I hope will have a big impact.

My final thanks goes to you, the reader, for taking your time to read this book and often to share it with your friends or loved ones, and to the many people who have taken the time to let me know how "Diving into the Deep" has impacted them. You have been a great encouragement to me.

ABOUT THE COVER

Roger Bansemer, our front cover designer, is a nationally recognized artist, and I am glad to count him as a good friend. You may recognize him from the PBS show, *Painting and Travel with Roger and Sarah Bansemer,* or from his many books, such as *Journey to Titanic.*

For a full introduction to Roger's work, visit www.bansemer.com.

Back Cover design by Jacquelyn Thayer: My image as a young boy in a sailor hat, imagining my future.

CONTENTS

INDEX OF CAPTAIN'S LOGS

The Captain's Logs primarily focus on experiences connected to the Titanic, *the Titanic Museums in Pigeon Forge, Tennessee and Branson, Missouri, and the expedition to the site of the* Titanic *in the North Atlantic.*

2017

Illumination Bronze Medal
Recipient

Sponsored by the Jenkins Group and *Independent Publisher* magazine, the Illumination Awards "celebrate and recognize the exemplary books produced by the ever-growing Christian branch of publishing and bookselling, bringing inspiration and answers to millions of readers exploring their faith."

Recipients were selected from hundreds of entries by a panel of judges. According to Jenkins Group, the awards "honor and bring increased recognition to the year's best new titles written and published with a Christian worldview." 2017 medalists include books from the United States, Canada, Australia, New Zealand, and South Africa, from long-established publishers, small presses, and self-published authors.

FOREWORD

When I am asked about Lowell, the key word I think of is *passion*. He cares about young people, sharing the Word of God, and telling the story of *Titanic*. We are honored by his portrayal of the *Titanic* captain at our Branson, Missouri, and Pigeon Forge, Tennessee museums.

You will never meet a kinder and more gentle person, and his writing reflects all of these elements. This book will inform and inspire you.

Mary Kellogg-Joslyn and the Titanic Crew

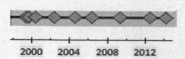

2000   2004   2008   2012

TITANIC ADVENTURE

When I was 66, adventure called me on the phone through the voice of my neighbor, Mark Lach. Over the years, I'd learned to recognize adventure's voice, but I must admit I was surprised to hear from him again after so much time had passed.

He didn't tell me all that was up ahead. If he had, I may not have had the courage to say "yes."

Instead, he just said, "Come," and I went! How could I resist?

What happened next is almost unimaginable.

INTRODUCTION

I've lived an extraordinary life, full of Victorian romance and swashbuckling adventure, gripping tragedy and hilarious comedy that has taken me literally around the world and both over and under the high seas. Through the past eighty years or so, I've experienced heart-wrenching losses and magnificent victories. Stomach-churning scenes have played out from my own precarious decisions and circumstances and the breath-taking magic of God's hand in my life.

All of these adventures have taught me the value of putting one's faith to the test, and sharing this story with you now is yet another opportunity to "dive into the deep." My hope and prayer is that you will learn something from both my experiences and my mistakes and that you would find courage to follow God's leading in your life in spite of your weaknesses, fears, or failures. I want you to experience what I have come to know as "faith rest," the ability to live your most abundant life, not by tremendous effort, but by tenacious trust.

Throughout this book, I will take you on a journey that started when I was a small boy and hasn't ended yet. Every time you read a Captain's Log you will be jumping back to my present and on-going adventure with the *Titanic*. Hopefully, you won't get seasick moving back and forth between the present and the past. As you read these stories, my hope is that you will find a way to allow God to be your Captain and that you would learn to follow His orders without hesitation, as if your very life depended on it.

It does.

Lowell Lytle

CAPTAIN'S LOG: THE SURFACE

Dateline: August 17, 2000 - ATLANTIC OCEAN
latitude 41° 43' 57" North, longitude 49° 56' 49" West

When we arrived at the surface, it was almost dark. We went through the normal process of having the cowboys hook us up to the crane and lift us to the deck. These men were called "cowboys" because it was their job to jump from their dinghy to the top of the small deep-water submersible, sometimes in very rough seas, like a rodeo rider on a bucking bull.

Cowboys hook the MIR to the crane to be hoisted on deck.[1]

We remained lodged in our tiny compartment, watching every move through the four-inch portals, as the crane slowly and meticulously lifted us out of the ocean and swung us around to set us down gingerly on deck. We waited, impatiently now, as the *MIR* was secured and the cables from the crane swung away. When the hatch was finally opened, we stepped out to a cheering crowd of about a hundred people—crew members, media, salvage specialists, historians, and other observers, as the

22

Emerging from the MIR²

conservator waited in his lab to see our bounty.

This all seemed so strange to me. I had been performing all my life, and it is quite normal to expect people to applaud when you finish your performance, but I had done nothing in the past twelve hours except visit one of the most breathtaking and remote sites in the world. If anything, I should be the one applauding the people who made it possible for me to go on that fantastic voyage.

Of course, the first thing I had to do when I got off the ladder was an interview with Fox Television. I'm an actor. You could put me in front of twenty thousand people, and I wouldn't be nervous.

But when they put that camera in my face and said, "What was it like, Mr. Lytle?" I was startled to realize that, when I answered, my voice was shaking. I don't think anyone else noticed it, but I did. You cannot see the *Titanic* with your own eyes and not be emotionally affected.

It didn't take long before we all gathered around the baskets to see what kind of treasure we had brought up. I think the item that moved me most was not from my dive, but the suitcase

Roger Bansemer viewing contents of the suitcase from the Titanic

that was brought up the next day on Roger Bansemer's dive.

When we opened it up, it was almost as if we could feel the soul of the original owner coming into that room. No one had seen the contents of that suitcase for more than eighty-eight years. In the suitcase were two pairs of men's shoes, size twelve (a work pair and a dress pair). There was a suit, a vest, two shirts, some underwear, socks, a cigarette lighter, a pocket watch, a cravat, and a few other items—all neatly folded. I was struck with the awareness that I was looking at someone's personal belongings. Who was this man? And did he survive?

Examining the contents of the suitcase recovered from the Titanic

These were questions we thought would never be answered... until someone noticed the initials "W.A." monogrammed on the inside of the shirts. We looked on the manifest, and there was one William Allen from England. He was 38 years old, a toolmaker from Birmingham, married for six years. His best friend, George Hinkley, had a job as a steward aboard the *Titanic* and probably talked his buddy William into buying a third-class steerage ticket. Imagine the plans they had made together for their visit to New York. William may have intended to find work in the United States and later send for his wife.

He didn't make it.

CHAPTER 1

CAPTAIN SMITH

TITANIC SINKS FOUR HOURS AFTER HITTING ICEBERG;
866 RESCUED BY CARPATHIA, PROBABLY 1250 PERISH;
ISMAY SAFE, MRS. ASTOR MAYBE, NOTED NAMES MISSING

How was it that, at 68 years of age, I was privileged to go on an expedition to see the final resting place of the *Titanic*? What improbable chain of events led me to this most haunting and desolate graveyard, and for what purpose? Just a few years earlier, I was struggling like many people in their sixties, not ready (nor financially able) to retire, looking for meaningful work, wondering how my wife and I were going to be able to overcome the many obstacles, physical and financial, that threatened our senior years. Yet, hadn't I learned over and over again that God always has a plan?

It should not have been a surprise, then, that at age 66 I was hired to portray Captain E.J. Smith at the first *Titanic* museum in Orlando, Florida. This was truly a dream job for me, and I soon learned that God had greater things in mind than simply giving an old seafarer a chance to act as captain of the *Titanic*.

People always ask me, "How did you get this job?" It's a good question. I saw James Cameron's movie *Titanic* like everyone else did, and I was amazed at how well it was done, but I was not a *Titanic* fanatic at all. *Titanic* was just another great movie. Like everyone else I had used the phrase "*Titanic* tragedy" to refer to anything big that fell apart; it meant nothing more to me.

One day, I was sitting at home when a phone call came from one of the designers of the new *Titanic* exhibit, an old friend of mine named Mark Lach. Mark said, "We have gone through three hundred and fifty actors, trying to find the right person for the captain, and we can't find him. I told the owners, 'I know someone that can play that part. He's my neighbor and lives right across the street from me.'"

Mark was much more than my neighbor; he grew up with my children and then became an instrumental part, literally, of an earlier musical adventure you will read about later in the book. So now my connection with him came full circle. I have learned never to be surprised when I see God pull together people and events in the strangest of ways to accomplish His goals.

I drove over to Orlando and met Mark. He took me into a room where six or seven men were sitting around a table and introduced me, saying, "Gentlemen, here's Captain E.J. Smith."

Newsboy sells copies of the Evening News, April 16, 1912 [27]

Front page of the April 16, 1912 edition of the New York Times

I had no idea what the captain looked like, and I hadn't gone prepared for an audition, and yet they all took one look at me and said "Yes … you're the one."

I spent the next few hours roaming around the exhibit and marveled at how well it was done. Toward the end of my tour, I went into the gift shop and saw the front page of a *New York Times* 1912 edition showing the photo of Captain E.J. Smith.

From fifteen feet away, my first impression was that Mark had taken my photo and pasted it on the front page of the *New York Times*. I thought to myself, "He shouldn't do that!" On closer look, I could see that it was not really me, but I could definitely see the resemblance.

I spent quite a bit of time in the next two years over at that exhibit, performing with the other actors and helping make the *Titanic* artifacts come alive. We each played our roles, visiting with the guests, telling them stories and answering their questions. For our occasional breaks, there was the customary green room, where we could lounge around and watch television or get something to eat. Once in a while, I would go into the gift shop, where they had a large high-back oak chair that was covered in red velvet and pushed right up next to the big plate glass windows that overlooked the passersby. Just for the fun of it, I would sit in that chair very still and watch the people stop and stare at me. They would place their noses against the glass and say, "I don't know... . He looks real... . He must be made of wax." After a few moments I would turn my body the other way and watch them jump back, totally startled. To me, that was entertaining.

It was also interesting to see the reaction of visitors when they would see me walking through the exhibit. You could tell that some of them were *Titanic* fanatics and were obviously aware of what Captain Smith had actually looked like. They would grab their heart, drop their jaw, breathe in, and look as if they had just seen a ghost. The exhibit was so well done that you felt like you were walking on board the real *Titanic*, and my resemblance to Captain Smith just completed the picture.

This stark likeness to Smith backfired on me once. I was on the bridge in the Branson, Missouri, exhibit, standing by the ship's wheel, when a lady came in with her 5-year-old boy. She said to him, "Do you want to shake the captain's hand?" He nodded his head, so I reached down and shook his little hand.

Then his mother said, "Can you find his picture over there on the wall?" There was a large picture of the captain and his officers that was probably five feet wide. The room was full of people, but the boy made his way through them to the picture. Sure enough, he was able to point to the captain. Then he turned his head to the left and looked at me again, then back to the picture. He looked back at me and said, "Did you die?"

I was quite taken aback by this question, wondering to myself, "What's going on in that little mind of his?" People do want to know if the captain died that day, and I always tell them the truth: yes, he did. But I probably should not have said that to a 5-year-old boy. Suddenly, he thought he was looking at a ghost. He came to me, wrapped his little thin arms around my legs, hugged me, and said, "I love you, and I'm going to miss you. I'll see you at the cemetery." He must have been to a cemetery not long before our encounter, perhaps saying goodbye to

Speaking with visitors at the Titanic museum

a grandparent, a friend, or some other family member. It took a lot of effort for me to keep myself together the rest of the day.

Captain Smith perished in the dark and icy North Atlantic on April 15, 1912, at the age of 62. He had been on the sea since he was 12. He left behind a wife and a 10-year-old daughter, who both, no doubt, loved and missed him.

In the *Titanic* museum, the ship's bridge and promenade deck were recreated to give the visitor a sense of the passengers' experience onboard. It was amazing: you could look over the bulwarks and see the water, the stars, and the constellations, just the way it all appeared to the passengers that fateful night. You could also see the distress rockets going up in the night sky. Mirrors on both sides of the room gave the illusion that you were actually walking on deck. The cool air, kept at 52°, added to the reality of this experience.

During the summertime in Florida, it gets fairly warm, as I'm sure most people know. When you're dressed up in a captain's uniform, even with air-conditioning, it still gets quite hot, so from time to time I would go out on the promenade deck to cool down and take refuge, while waiting for another group to come through. One day, the actor who was portraying Mr. Thomas, the designer of the *Titanic*, came out on deck with the shipbuilding plans in hand. He said to me, "I've got an idea. Let's do some improv and pretend we just struck the iceberg!"

That sounded like a great idea to me, much more enjoyable than just following the same old script, so I said, "Let's go!"

We barged in through the bridge room, right next to the promenade deck. In the room were the ship's wheel, telegraph apparatus, and a sheet of ice replicating an iceberg. There were around forty-five people in the room, studying the artifacts and putting their hands on the iceberg. I said, "Are you sure, Mr. Andrews?"

"Yes, E.J.," he answered, "I've gone below, and six of the bulkheads are torn open. If just four were flooded, we could make it, but not with all six."

I walked over to the table, placed the plans on it, and pointed to them. "What about the water pumps?"

He said, "They will keep us afloat for a while, but it's a mathematical certainty that within an hour and forty minutes or so the ship will founder."

By this time, the people had gathered around us in a little circle. I shook my head and said, "It looks like Ismay's going to get his headlines after all" (a reference to the chairman of White Star Lines, the company that built the *Titanic*). Ismay had reportedly ordered the captain to push the *Titanic* in order to reach New York by Wednesday evening for a party, and he was also found responsible for trimming the number of lifeboats on board the ship, a fateful choice made in favor of a more spacious promenade.

Now I looked up at the guests gathered around and shouted, "People, get aboard the lifeboats IMMEDIATELY!" All forty-five of them ran to get out on deck, pushing and shoving to get through the door. The deck was packed with people and, of course, there were no life boats, so what should I do now? Well, when you're doing improvisation, you have to think on your feet. I leaned over the railing and shouted to a pretend crew member, "Where are the lifeboats?"

"They're on the starboard side," came back the answer (but I had shouted back this answer myself, using a ventriloquism technique learned in my youth). Now I turned and shouted to the people, "The life boats are on the starboard side. Women and children, get to the other side of the ship and get into the lifeboats!" Mr. Andrews started separating the women and children.

Within a few moments, two of the actresses happened to come on deck. They could see what we were doing and immediately joined in. They took the women and children into the other room, where they had a life belt on display, and left me with sixteen men. I had no idea what I was going to say next, and neither did Mr. Andrews.

Because it was 52° in that room, and the men were all dressed for 94° Florida weather, I didn't want to hold them there too long. After a short pause, I said, "What's the last thing you said to your loved one? Have you told them you loved them today? You know we're all going to die sometime, and whenever it happens, it will be too soon." As I spoke, the strains of "Nearer My God to Thee" were being played by a string quartet in stereophonic sound above our heads. Suddenly, it all became very real for those sixteen men.

For the next three or four minutes, I talked to them about life in general and how important it is that we communicate with our loved

Posing with fellow actors on the Grand Staircase at the Orlando Exhibit

ones on a day-to-day basis. I ended by saying, "The next time you see your loved one, let them know how much you love them."

I had no idea that Mr. Andrews was telling the women and children in the other room exactly the same thing. When I opened the door and let the men out, they rushed over to their women and put their arms around them. The women had tears running down their cheeks. I can assure you: THOSE PEOPLE GOT THEIR MONEY'S WORTH!

Mr. Andrews and I did the same routine several times that day. Once, when he wasn't available, I foolishly thought to myself, "I can do this on my own. I don't need him." There were about fifteen people out on deck when I barged through the door and shouted, "Mr. Andrews has informed me that we just struck an iceberg, and within an hour and a half, this ship will be on the ocean floor. All women and children, get aboard the lifeboats. Gentlemen, we will have to fend for ourselves." With that, a little girl screamed and threw up on the deck. That was the last time we did that act.

I have many more stories to tell you about my experiences portraying the captain of the *Titanic*. Every time you see "Captain's Log," I'll be sharing the best of them with you, but I have another story to tell you that is far more intriguing and quite unbelievable. It's a true account about a completely incredible journey to the high seas, a journey I have taken more than once, an adventure you, too, can embark on with little more than your own willingness to go.

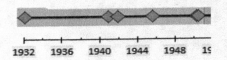

Preparing for
the Voyage

They say the person you are in second grade is your true self, the person you should look to later in life when you are questioning your path. Amidst childhood scenes that could have been lifted out of a "Little Rascals" movie, these were the defining events of my youth, experiencesthat would teach me much of what I needed to know about my own calling.

To understand the adventures that follow, you must take a look back at where and how they all began.

Imagine you are watching
these scenes play out on a
vintage black-and-white
television set with poor
reception, and remember
these stories, since
elements from each of
them will reemerge
later in the story.

I had no idea
I was preparing
for something so
unimaginable!

CHAPTER 2

A STONE'S THROW

I was just 6 years old, standing in my parents' bedroom against the west wall. My mother was facing me on the opposite side of the room, and she started to throw stones at me. I couldn't believe it! My dear mother was throwing stones at me. Why would she do that? Actually, I knew why, but I was still in shock, begging her to stop. She loved me, and I knew it, but there she was throwing stones at her own son. She intentionally hit me only once, in the leg, but each stone terrified me, and I cried my heart out. What was going on? I'll tell you, but allow me to begin at the beginning.

It was 1938, and our country was well into the Great Depression. Like most families, we didn't have a great deal to eat and got by with only the necessities. Yes, I'm one of those kids who had to walk to school in the snow a mile and a half one way with holes in my shoes, and then I had to make the same journey back home. I cut pieces of cardboard out of breakfast cereal boxes and slipped them into my shoes to cover the holes, so that my feet would not get wet.

During those trying years, my father worked wherever he could, mostly in the coal industry or in sales. Eventually he got a job working for the United States Unemployment Office. It didn't pay much, but he was glad to have a job. Almost no one escaped the threat of losing their livelihood in those dark days, and our family was no exception.

As the years went by, I don't believe Dad ever realized that the Depression was over. He was forever frugal when buying food. During the Depression itself, he did all the grocery shopping and would bring home things like soybean steaks or cans of grits. It really didn't help much that Mom wasn't a very good cook.

Our home on 20th Street in Jackson, Michigan, still looking much as it did in the 1930s

I don't remember a lot about my father from my early years, but I do remember that he would come home from work and then sit in his chair and read a newspaper. At 5:30 he would say, "Gladys, it's time to eat." She would go into the kitchen, turn the stove on high, put the frying pan on, and then throw in some liver (or whatever else we happened to have at the time) and cook it until it was dried and curled up. She served these "meals" right out of the frying pan. I never enjoyed eating much until after I got married.

I was born in Kalamazoo, Michigan, but when I was very young, our family moved to a small town called Jackson. We moved from house to house a lot there in Jackson, but the place I think of as home was on the outskirts of town, on a gravel road called 20th Street. Our house was a blue bungalow on top of a hill. It was in my parents' bedroom in that house that I found myself facing Mom's punishment. Earlier in the day, I had thrown stones at my older brother, Terry, and I must have gotten a lucky shot in. Or perhaps I was just not as clever as Terry at staying out of Mom's sights. Frustrated at being bullied and picked on by him all day every day and feeling powerless against his taunts, I was angry.

Terry was four years older and loved to tease me, as older brothers do. I was too small to hit him with my fists. He would just grab me and squeeze me into a little ball. That day I looked around to see if anyone was watching, closed my fist around a stone on the ground, and then flung it at him. When the stone hit its mark, I sent another and another his way, finally finding a way to get back at him from a distance... until, that is, I was caught.

Mother was very creative when it came to correcting us and teaching us things, and she didn't often resort to taking this kind of approach. I never forgot the feeling of being so vulnerable and alone in that moment.

It was not that Terry and I didn't love each other; we did. We had to; there was no one else to play with. Of course, being four years older, he was a little sharper than I was, so he usually won the day.

My relationship with Terry was pivotal to the events that followed, so I need to share some stories that may take you back to your own childhood or give you a window into a very different era. You will see that, although Terry and I had a typical sibling rivalry, we did love each other and would ultimately follow each other, literally, to the ends of the earth.

When Terry was young, he had a bad case of asthma. His sinuses drained continually, and at any given moment he could hock up a giant, stringy mess we called a loogey. He would pin me down on

With my older brother Terry in 1940

41

the bed and let a loogey slowly string down from his lips right over my face. Then, just before it broke loose, he would suck it back up. I was forced to lie there with my head turning from side to side, because he had my shoulders pinned. You get the picture.

Well, he did this trick one too many times. One day, he couldn't bring this slimy mess back up, and it landed right in my face. I had definite thoughts that day as to how Mom should correct him. I think she did give him a spanking, and he certainly had it coming.

We loved playing cops and robbers, running around the house and yelling, "BANG!" with our pointed fingers pulled out of our imaginary holsters. Of course, Terry always seemed to shoot me first. One day I managed to sneak up on him and gleefully shouted, "BANG! BANG!"

I was overjoyed... until he turned around and shouted, "I filled your gun with blanks!" Deflated, I had no answer for that.

Terry and I did a lot of projects together. If we weren't making water cascades on the hillside, we would scrape a miniature golf course out of the dirt in the woods and field next to our house. One Christmas, we made a snowman that looked like Santa Claus. Inside of him, we placed a two-way speaker I had won in a radio contest, and when anyone came by, Santa Claus would seem to be talking to them. No one had ever seen anything like it before. What fun that was!

Even when we were very young children, it seemed as though our parents took us to every church service or prayer meeting happening any night of the week in Jackson or the nearby towns. They were anxious for us to make a personal decision to become followers of Jesus and develop spiritual disciplines as early in life as possible.

During Wednesday night prayer meetings, Terry and I were on our knees in the pews for what seemed like hours, looking at old ladies' legs and wondering how long it would be before we could go home.

Many times, on the way back home, we would ask Dad to stop at the filling station so that we could get some *Guess What?*s. *Guess What?*s were small boxes with a piece of candy and a toy inside of them. Dad would protest, "You don't want to get that. It's made in Japan, and someday they're going to take those pennies, turn them into bullets, and shoot our boys."

Just a few months later, he would be proved right, but you know how boys can be. We kept insisting, "Come on, Dad! PLEASE!" In the end, he would give in.

We knew our parents were always praying for us, especially our mother, waiting patiently for the right time to share God's plan of salvation with us. By the time I was 7, Terry had already received Christ. One particular summer evening, Mom could wait no longer. After dinner, she sat me down at the living room couch, taking her time to point out several scripture verses to me, walking me step-by-step through those simple truths in a way that I could understand.

I remember that it was about twenty minutes after seven in the evening because Dad said, "Hurry up, Gladys, *The Lone Ranger* comes on in ten minutes." Priorities are priorities. (For those who don't remember *The Lone Ranger*, it was a radio program that came on every week night at 7:30, probably the most famous radio show of the late 1930s and 40s.)

After I had invited Christ into my life, I felt like a new person. It must have been a real conversion, because the first thing I wanted to do was to help Mom do dishes instead of listening to *The Lone Ranger*.

Mom wasted no time in teaching me the importance of sharing God's Good News with others. The very next day, when the milkman and mailman came to our door, she handed me a Gospel tract and said, "Go give it to him, Lowey." Her passion and urgency about sharing Jesus with as many people as possible made a lasting impression on both Terry and me.

Mother was a very creative person. She would take us both to the window every night and say, "Look out there at the sky. Those clouds could open up any minute, and Jesus could come. Listen for a trumpet to sound, for the Lord could come back at any time!"

She would add, "You see those lights in the houses out there? Those people don't know about Jesus, and it's up to us to tell them." Night after night, we would look up at the sky and think about the people living in those houses. She instilled in both of us a strong sense of duty to reach the lost, something all Christians everywhere should do.

Even though Terry and I wanted to do right, as Mom tried so hard to teach us during those early years, like any kids we always seemed to get into trouble anyway.

During one of our family moves, we had to go meet our prospective landlords. It was a natural thing for a landlord to check out a family before renting them an apartment. While Dad was talking to the couple, Terry and I noticed that in their kitchen they had a birdcage with a parrot in it. We asked the landlords if we could go and see it, and when they said yes, we took off running for the kitchen.

Dad stopped us in our tracks, saying, "Boys, come back here. You know better than to walk in front of people." We went back to where we started, got down on our hands and knees, and crawled past them to the kitchen.

We didn't get the apartment.

Any time Terry and I did something bad, Mom would say, "Just wait till your Dad gets home." The minute Dad came in the door each evening he would ask, "What did the boys do wrong today?" He whipped us with his belt, as many fathers did in that era.

When Mom whipped us herself, she would make us go out and cut a switch from a nearby tree. I would always get the smallest one I could find. I never seemed to catch on that it was the thin ones that stung the most. After I found one I liked and brought it in, she would slowly take off all the leaves except those on the very end of the switch. All the while, I would be jumping up and down, anticipating the pain that was about to come. She left those last few leaves on so that I could hear the swat coming, as well as feel it when it landed.

Eventually, Dad got a better job selling calendars, rubber stamps, and office supply items to businesses around Jackson, and we moved to a home on Euclid Street.

When Christmas time came around, Terry and I were always well-behaved playmates, just in case Santa was watching. I remember well the Christmas we ran down the stairs and saw a tree with more presents than usual under it and a model train set circling around them.

Another year, Terry got a Silver King bicycle—and I didn't. The

body of the Silver King was made of aluminum. It was a real beauty, and I was so jealous. My parents explained that Terry had to have a better bicycle because he needed to earn money by delivering newspapers.

Priorities are priorities.

Like any brothers, there was always a sense of competition and jealousy between us. I had always looked up to Terry, but this part of our relationship caused many struggles through the years. I learned many years later that God will use everything, even our personal issues, to advance His Gospel.

So many of our memories are hilarious. One Halloween, I was invited to a party next door, but I had no costume to wear, and we couldn't afford the costumes being sold in the dime store. My creative mother put charcoal on my face, put a hat sideways on my head and a turnip in my right hand, and said, "Go over there, shake that and enjoy yourself." I thought it was a pretty goofy idea, but I had nothing else, so I went to the party with that turnip in my hand, shaking it. I must have looked like the bogeyman, judging by the way everyone stared at me.

Mom's creativity went a little too far sometimes. For instance, she was always afraid that we would catch cold at night, so she pinned our covers over us with giant horse blanket pins (which were about five inches long). When my cousins would come over to spend the night, she would pin them in, too. Needless to say, they didn't come over very often.

The most pivotal moment of my early childhood was, of course, the day I accepted Christ, but not long after that I discovered something else that would shape my future dramatically. During all of those church services and prayer meetings, there was a lot of singing. I learned most of the songs by heart, even though I didn't yet know what all the words meant. In the early 40s, when a revival came to town, meetings would go on for weeks at a time. The Humbard Family Singers, a family music group from Ohio that eventually became known as Rex Humbard Ministries, came to Jackson shortly after I became a Christian and stayed for two whole months. Our family was there for every service. I didn't mind going so much because I fell in love with the bass player, a pretty little brunette, but it must have been hard for Dad to miss *The Lone Ranger* for eight weeks in a row!

One particular afternoon during the months those meetings were going on, I remember sitting on the floor against the wall in the dining room, watching while Mom ironed clothes. She started to sing a song about Grace:

Marvelous grace of our loving Lord,

Grace that exceeds our sin and our guilt!

Yonder on Calvary's mount outpoured,

There where the blood of the Lamb was spilled.

Grace, grace, God's grace,

Grace that will pardon and cleanse within;

Grace, grace, God's grace,

Grace that is greater than all our sin![3]

I loved to listen to Mom sing; but this day, as she sang, I started to sing along with her, and I was singing harmony. We were both shocked. I didn't know I could do that, and she didn't either. This early recognition that I had a talent and an ear for music was a critical moment in my life.

CAPTAIN'S LOG:
THINGS DON'T ALWAYS WORK
RIGHT ON THE *TITANIC*

Dateline: Summer 1999 - TORONTO, CANADA

The items that were on display in Orlando's *Titanic* museum in the late 1990s were originally found floating on the surface of the ocean by the crew of the CS *Mackay-Bennett*, the ship sent to collect bodies immediately after the tragedy. In 1987, the first salvage dive to the *Titanic* succeeded in retrieving over fifteen hundred items from the wreckage. Since that time, about four thousand more artifacts have been retrieved, among them a set of the *Titanic*'s gigantic steam whistles. In 1999, a *Titanic* exhibit, including those original whistles, was set up for display in Toronto, Canada, and I was asked to go there to meet with the media to promote the exhibit.

I had to go three days in advance of the big opening, and each day I went around to the various television and radio stations, promoting what was to be a special event to announce the opening of the exhibition. At exactly 12 noon on Saturday in the town square, they were to blow *Titanic*'s whistles again. My job was to see if I could pack in a crowd for this kickoff event.

At each radio and television station, I would talk about the wonderful artifacts and how LOUD those whistles would be. I had been told they were the largest whistles ever made and that when they were first fired off in Belfast, Ireland, you could hear them eleven miles away. The actual whistles were sounded again in St. Paul, Minnesota, earlier that same year (on February 20). Using compressed air instead of steam, they fired off two ten-second blasts, while an estimated one

With one of Titanic's restored whisiles in Toronto, Canada

hundred thousand people watched and listened to The Voice of the *Titanic*.

Saturday rolled around, and someone picked me up at my hotel around 11 o'clock in the morning to take me to the town square. When we got there, about 11:15, the place was already filled with people. They drove me behind a large platform where I was to speak. The back of the stage had been draped with a large, heavy black cloth approximately ten feet high. Behind the cloth there was a huge boiler that was to be used to fire up the whistles. The whistles themselves stood on a pole approximately twelve feet above the ground at the far end of the stage. I was told that they would use eight men to fire up the boiler and produce enough pressure to blow those massive whistles.

I was to introduce several celebrities and dignitaries: a singer, a famous skier, an actor, the mayor, and someone from the United Way. Just before I went on stage, the event manager said to me, "Oh, by the way, we have a slight problem. The conservator says we cannot blow the real whistles today. He inspected them last night and found that the insides were damaged the last time they were blown. So we have put some replica whistles up there on that pole. The real whistles are down here in front, so if people want to come up and look at them and take pictures, they can. Would you be so kind as to announce this?"

I thought to myself, "Are you kidding? These people have been promised that they would hear the real whistles, and now I have to get up there and tell them they can't?" I wasn't looking forward to that at all!

Now, try to picture this: it was a beautiful September day, not a cloud in the sky. I was on the stage overlooking approximately three thousand people, with at least twenty television cameras aimed in my direction. This was to be a big, LIVE media event, broadcast from the Atlantic to the Pacific, something like *Good Morning America.*

I started out by giving the people gathered a warm welcome, and then I said, "You know, things don't always work right on the *Titanic*," and I told them what had happened. Amazingly no one expressed any disappointment at making the trip to hear a replica instead of the real whistles.

Before I could finish introducing the special guests, I could feel a mist falling on me and noticed that all the television cameras had turned and were now aimed at the whistles. I glanced up to my left and saw steam pouring out of them. I quickly grabbed the microphone and moved to my right, trying to escape the moisture and finish the introductions. Steam continued to billow out of the whistles, and the excitement mounted.

"People," I shouted, "I believe it's about time to blow the whistles. So get ready! It's going to be EXTREMELY LOUD! Put your hands over your ears and help me count down." Turning to face the whistles, I began: "Here we go now—5 … 4 … 3 … 2 … 1!" Nothing happened! A few seconds later I heard something that sounded like someone had sat on a somewhat deflated "whoopee cushion." And that was it. I couldn't believe it! You could hardly hear whatever it was that came out of that thing from more than two hundred feet away.

My back was still to the audience, and I did not want to turn around and face them, but I knew I had to. I spun around now and said with all the confidence I could muster: "AND THERE YOU HAVE IT! GIVE TO THE UNITED WAY, AND SEE THE *TITANIC* EXHIBIT!" and I turned to run from the stage, and many in the crowd turned to go, too.

The event manager stopped me and said, "No! No! The lever got caught on a nail. We're doing it one more time."

I ran back to the microphone. "Come back, people!" I said.

"We're going to try it one more time. The lever got caught on a nail." Those who had already started to leave turned and came back. (Canadians are very forgiving folks.) I shouted to the men in the back who were working with the boiler: "Do you have enough steam built up?"

"Yes!" they shouted back.

"All right, folks," I began again, "put your hands over your ears and count down with me now. 3 ... 2 ... 1..."

BLA-A-A-T! This time was worse than before. I got off the stage as quickly as I could and ran behind the drapes, hoping no one would follow me. But, no! The TV cameras were hot on my trail. Things don't always work right on the *Titanic*.

Although that day was definitely an embarrassing experience for me, it certainly wasn't my first time to be embarrassed. Those memories go way back...

CHAPTER 3

A PENNY WAITING FOR CHANGE

Like many fathers during the Great Depression, Dad struggled to provide for us, and we had to move often from one place to another, to avoid creditors and the disgrace of being evicted by the sheriff. The next residence we came to (hoping it would be the last) was an unusually large house by our standards. On moving day, when we pulled up in front of 326 Clinton Street and I looked out the window of our car, I was surprised to see a great big house.

Running inside excitedly to check things out, I first went to the living room. It didn't seem to be anything special. I ran to the kitchen, and there was nothing special about it either. Next, I went down a small connecting hallway and entered what I thought had to be a bedroom, and what did my eyes behold? It was a real bunk bed! WOW! Golly! Gee whiz. I really didn't say these things because we weren't allowed to use slang words, but that's what I was thinking.

As I was caressing the top bunk (that would certainly be mine), out of the corner of my eye I caught sight of an imposing dark structure outside of the window next to me. What was this? Could it be a barn? It was. Suddenly all of the scenarios of life with my bothersome brother were pushed to the side, and I began to wonder what worlds lay before me inside that mysterious wooden cathedral. This move wasn't going to be so bad, after all!

I was in third grade now, and it was December again, time to prepare for Christmas. What would Christmas be like this year? We went to our cousins' home because they always had the greatest Christmas tree. I had never seen anything like it before. It was huge! The only thing I didn't understand was why Uncle Cornell always cut the top of

the tree off. Almost two thirds of the way up, he would just lop it off. I would always jokingly go upstairs to see if the top of the tree had been pushed through the ceiling.

Uncle Cornell had to be a rich man. His children got more presents than you could imagine. And their tree... WOW! What a tree! It had angel hair and icicles all over it, with more lights than I had ever seen.

Somehow, the Christmas tree we always got had to be put together in pieces. Dad would drill holes in the trunk and jam tree branches into those holes and then wire them in place. This year, however, would be different. We had no money for a Christmas tree at all. My third-grade teacher had a Christmas tree at the back of our classroom, and on the last day before our Christmas vacation, she asked if there was anyone who did not have a Christmas tree at home. I raised my hand, but so did another girl. After class, we tossed a coin to see who would get the tree. Unfortunately, I won.

It was a spruce tree that, by then, had been standing alongside a heater for three weeks. By the time I had dragged it all the way home, there was not a needle left on it. It looked worse than a Charlie Brown tree. It still had the shape of a tree, large at the bottom and small at the top, so we put it in the corner and covered every branch with icicles, hoping that no one would notice there were no needles on it.

It didn't work. When my cousin came over and saw the tree, he said, "Holy gee, what happened to your tree?" I felt like a penny waiting for change. That next year we went out and bought a nice Christmas tree, the kind with all its needles intact. Dad still took it down to the basement, drilled holes in the trunk, and jammed in more branches.

Throughout my childhood I was a skinny kid, and I hated it. I followed all the Jack Armstrong training rules, but it didn't help. Jack Armstrong was a popular comic book character who also had his own radio show. He was always going on great adventures, and it was the desire of every boy my age to be just like Jack Armstrong.

On the back page of one of my comic books, there was a picture of a muscular man kicking sand in the face of a thin man and then walking off with his girlfriend. I thought to myself, "Yup, that's going to be me."

I was already a very insecure kid, and being skinny didn't help. In fact, I looked so unhealthy that my parents put me in an "open-air" school in Jackson. This was a special school for children who were sickly or in danger of contracting tuberculosis, a crippling illness before a vaccine was invented to prevent it. Open-air schools were sprouting up all over the country, following the belief that the only thing children needed to bolster their health was more fresh air. Teachers would open the windows wide, even in the wintertime, hoping to improve our health. It didn't work. I just got cold.

By the time I reached fourth grade, all I wanted was a friend who looked as unhealthy as I did, and I found one. His name was Harley Jones, and he reminded me of the kid who put his tongue on the frozen pole in the movie, *A Christmas Story*. In fact, that whole film reminded me of my life back then. I was about the same age as Ralphy—9. My dad had problems with the furnace, just like his dad did. The difference was that my Dad didn't swear. In *A Christmas Story*, there was a bully named Scut Farkus, and Harley and I had a bully in our elementary school, too. His name was George Wright. George was bigger than I was, and he picked on me all the time. He loved to pin my arm behind my back until I finally yelled, "Uncle! Uncle!"

Harley and I got hold of a little booklet that showed some jujitsu moves, and we practiced them on each other during recess. One day after lunch, I was standing in front of the classroom, getting ready to take my seat, when George came up to pick on me in front of the whole class. I got up enough courage to try a jujitsu move on him. I grabbed his left hand and twisted it back. At the same time, I put my leg behind his, and he went flying across the floor, sliding into the blackboard. Just then, Mrs. Chisholm came in and saw the whole thing. She pointed her finger at me and said, "Lowell, you'll have to stay after school." YES! For once, I was the bully!

Harley stayed with me after school that day. After about a half hour, Mrs. Chisholm said, "You can go home now."

But I didn't want to go. I knew George would be outside waiting for us, and I was sure he was going to kill us if he possibly could. I said, "No, I'll stay a little longer. I can clean up the erasers for you."

After another fifteen minutes, the teacher ordered us: "Go home! NOW!" Harley and I took off running down the hall at full speed and hit the exit door, and sure enough, George was right there waiting for us. We ran as fast as we could for two blocks uphill, then down to Perrine Street, then right two houses to Harley's house. All this time ol' Georgie was right on our tail.

We ran up the porch steps into Harley's house and into his mother's bedroom and closed the door. There was another door that opened onto the same front porch. It had no doorknob, but it did have a hole we could look out of. Harley grabbed his BB gun and shoved it through that hole, and when Georgie started up the steps, Harley started firing. Georgie turned and started running away, and we went out of the house after him. As we ran, Harley kept pumping BBs at George's legs. Ol' Georgie never bothered us again.

Chapter 4

First Kiss

The first girl I ever kissed sat right behind me in Mrs. Chisholm's room. I don't understand what I saw in Erma. She was kind of homely and had boogers in her eyes, but what can I say? It happened.

During one recess, we were all on the playground together. I don't remember everything that happened. What I do remember is that I was standing with my back against a fence, looking at the swing set, and in between me and the swing set stood Erma.

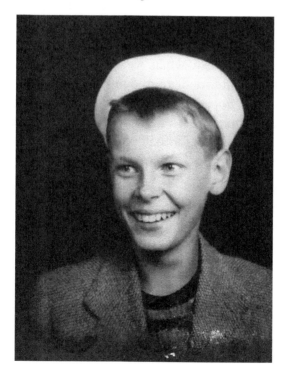

Do you remember what it was like when there was a fight on the playground? Everyone gathered around in a big circle and started to cheer for one person or the other. In that same vein, all of our classmates circled around and started shouting, "Kiss her, Lowell! Kiss her!"

I just stood there like I was frozen in the corner of a boxing ring, not knowing what to do. Then, the bell rang, and something is supposed to happen when the bell rings. I'm not sure if someone pushed me, or if I did it on my own, but I lunged forward and kissed her. My kiss fell on her nose. I missed her mouth completely.

As fate would have it, Mrs. Chisholm was standing at the window and saw the whole thing. Now we all had to line up to go back to class, and of course we had to walk by Mrs. Chisholm. I made sure I was the last one in line, hoping that she would leave for the classroom before I got to the door. But no! She stayed to the very end, and when I walked by her, she leaned over and said, "Lowell, was that necessary?" I just shook my head and marched meekly back to class.

That night, Erma called our house. Mom answered the phone and called out, "Lowell, your girlfriend's on the phone." I was so embarrassed. From then on, I never liked poor Erma. I had two more years of her sitting behind me in class, and two more years of Mrs. Chisholm, too. Fortunately, when we left elementary school, Erma went to a different intermediate and high school. I was so glad. I thought to myself, "I hope I never see that girl again." When I went to my fortieth class reunion, there she was, sitting right across from me. She had married one of the football players from my high school. At least there were no more boogers in her eyes!

In those days, conservative Christian parents did not allow their children to go to movie theaters, an obstacle which would later prove to be very ironic for my brother Terry and me, as movie going continued to grow in popularity. In fact, my first vision for our barn was to turn it into a theater where I could show cartoons. Somehow, in the middle of the Great Depression, Dad found a way to fulfill my impossible dream. On my birthday, I came home from school to find a 16mm projector sitting on the dining room table. I couldn't believe my eyes! This dream might happen yet!

A new friend of mine who had lots of 16mm cartoons lent me all of his reels to show. I made lots of posters of Mickey Mouse, Donald Duck, and the other cartoon characters and plastered them all over the building. I also showed a few films to friends and neighbors on the first floor of that barn-turned-theater before that particular dream fizzled, but a seed was planted in my childhood that would grow into an almost unbelievable adventure many years later.

Our family's favorite form of entertainment was the radio. We would sit around that little box with its tiny dim, light and listen to all kinds of dramatic theater. One day, an announcement from President Roosevelt himself interrupted our program: "Yesterday, December 7, 1941—a day which will live in infamy—the United States of America was suddenly and deliber-ately attacked by naval and air forces of the Empire of Japan."

By the next day, all the papers screamed the headlines: we were at war. I thought to myself, "Dad was sure right," and I felt a little guilty having eaten all those *Guess What?*s that made money for the Japanese manufacturers.

I made a lot of model airplanes during World War II. They were all made out of balsa wood, not like the plastic models of today. The thought came to me: "If I blow these plans up, I could make a much larger airplane, one that I could actually get inside of. Dad gave me permission to use a stack of 1x2s he had in the basement, so I dragged them up to the second story of the barn and began to frame up a fuselage that would be eight feet long.

I found a whole stack of 4x8 sheets of tin in the woods about two city blocks from our house. Someone had discarded them, so I dragged them all home and used them to cover the fuselage, rudder, and tail. My plane looked *great*, and I could actually crawl inside of it. The only thing I needed now was enough wood for some wings, but I never was able to find it.

Later on, Terry helped me cut a hole in the side of the barn and, using a block and tackle, we lowered my wingless plane to the ground, dragged it into the woods, and hung it in a tree, so that all the neighbor kids could use it as a swing.

That was another barn-spun dream that never quite made it, but definitely a sign of things to come. Just a few years later, Terry and I found ourselves working together on a building project of gigantic proportions, and much later in life, I was to build a different sort of vessel, on a very grand scale, and the seeds of it were most likely sown in the loft of that barn on Clinton Street.

Harley and I formed an Air Force club we called "The Black Cats." There was just the two of us in it, but we thought it was special, and we met every day after school in Dad's coal bin. Because Jackson was not far from Willow Run, a factory used to build war ships, we knew we would be a potential enemy target. Air-raid sirens would go off monthly in those days, and each neighborhood's air raid warden was responsible for checking every house to be sure lights were turned off and everyone was safely hidden away in the homemade bunkers.

During the day, Harley and I would scan the skies, ready to identify any German or Japanese planes that might be flying overhead. This was made possible because during the war you could buy fighter plane silhouette posters for the wall or a deck of cards with all the types of planes on them.

Everyone was on the alert in those days, and Harley and I were ready for action. We always dressed in makeshift Army Air Corp uniforms. Mrs. Chisholm let us wear them all day in class. We even had goggles, headsets, and little lead wings we pinned to our chests. I had fashioned these by melting lead on Mom's stove and pouring it into a mold I carved from a potato.

World War II cardboard cockpit simulator

Harley and I were anxious to do our part for the war effort, so we "taught" ourselves how to fly using a cardboard cockpit simulator that we bought at a local store. It was a full-sized simulator that accurately mimicked the controls of a military fighter. We practiced every night after school diligently, looking forward to our opportunity to stick it to the enemy. Nobody would allow two scrawny fourth graders to enlist, so we hatched a scheme to go down to the sporting goods store, grab some guns, and proceed to the airport where we "knew" we could commandeer a piper cub airplane and fight the enemy in the air. With the bravado of two determined 9-year-old boys, we actually believed we could fly a plane, while shooting out of the windows at the same time.

Though we never tried to actually follow our scheme to fight the enemy in the air, Harley and I did think it would be a good idea if we cut a hole in the roof of the barn (where I'd built my tin fuselage) so that we could see if any Germans or Japanese were flying over. The only threat that flew over was Dad, and he was flying mighty low that day. That ended our Air Force club.

Not long after that, Dad tore the barn down, but by then important seeds had been planted in me that were the result of all those hours of imaginative fun under its old rafters. These were seeds that would grow into my life's work and aid me in reaching thousands upon thousands of people for Christ.

My son David gave me a wonderful birthday present when I turned 70. He bought me a ticket to fly a World War II bird, a T-6. It was an

Preparing to take flight in a World War II T-6

authentic trainer. He paid the extra dollars so that I could actually do loops, barrel rolls, and other maneuvers. As I did, I couldn't help but think of Harley Jones.

Sometimes, Terry and I would play football with the neighbor kids out in the street, and once in a while the football would bounce into Old Lady Powell's front yard. She lived right across the street from us. Whenever this would happen, she would call the police on us. They would come by and say to us, "Don't worry about it. When we leave, just go back to playing." But she kept calling them.

The corner of Mrs. Powell's property line stuck about two feet into the area we used to slide down the hill in the wintertime, and occasionally the runners from our sleds would go over that line. But Old Lady Powell simply wouldn't have it. One day, she stacked ten or fifteen huge boulders on her corner. When we would come sliding down the hill, we could usually miss the boulders if we stayed to the left, but every now and then we would hit them and end up with a bloody nose or some broken teeth.

Terry and I decided to fix her good. We went down in the basement of our house and found several buckets of leftover paint in all kinds of colors. Then, at night, the two of us snuck out and painted those rocks. They were gaudy: orange with purple polka dots, bright green with yellow stripes. It looked just awful, but Mrs. Powell never painted over them.

The war was still on, and Mrs. Powell had a service flag in her window with two blue stars on it. Every mother with a son in the war effort was given a service flag to display, with one star for each son in service. One day, I saw that one of the blue stars in Mrs. Powell's flag had been replaced with gold. We knew what that meant: one of her sons had been killed in action. We never bothered Mrs. Powell again.

The misadventures of my childhood were never-ending, yet despite the struggles every American family felt during the war, it was a great era in which to grow up, and ours was a way of life long gone from American culture today.

I was just an ordinary child, although with debilitating insecurities and troubles. I made childish mistakes, took childish risks, and got into lots of childish trouble. But at the same time, some of my own personal gifts and talents began to emerge, and my spiritual foundation was established, with some of my deepest spiritual lessons learned during those early, impressionable years.

Summers with Dad taught me some particularly important lessons. He had a large tent, and we would go camping in the warmer weather, usually at Little Wolf Lake, one of many lakes that dotted Michigan's landscape (more than a hundred in our county alone). He liked this particular little lake, probably because it was less visited than most and, therefore, a great fishing spot. He would set up the tent, and we would go fishing all week.

I loved to fish, and I still do. It seemed as though Dad would always catch a dogfish because we became known as The Dogfish Lytles. Apparently, the dogfish were not good to eat because Dad always threw them in the trash. Still, our many fishing trips taught me a lesson that ultimately led me far from my little home in Jackson, Michigan, and straight into the greatest adventures of my life: "Fish where the fish are." One summer, we went camping out at the Gull Lake Bible Conference, and my parents brought home two plaster plaques to hang on the wall. One of them read, "Only one life, 'twill soon be past. Only what's done for Christ will last."[5]

I saw that plaque almost every day, and at critical moments in my life, that simple reminder helped me through some of my most difficult decisions. In this way, it has made a huge impact on my life.

The other plaque read, "Have you prayed about it?" These are two good thoughts worthy of being displayed in any home. One day, I had lost some keys somewhere in the front yard. I can't remember what those keys unlocked, but it was important that they be found. I looked all afternoon, spending many hours, and still couldn't find them. Finally, I went inside the house, very discouraged, and happened to see that plaque that read, "Have you prayed about it?" I thought to myself, "I haven't." In that moment, I stopped and prayed that God would give me wisdom to find the keys. I walked back out the front door, down the steps, and went right to the spot where the keys were lying. I learned early in life that prayer changes things.

CAPTAIN'S LOG: BAD LUCK IN ATLANTIC CITY

Dateline: Fall 1999 - ATLANTIC CITY, NEW JERSEY

I was asked to go to Atlantic City for the opening of a *Titanic* exhibit in one of their casinos. (In 2012, Hurricane Sandy swept through the area and destroyed many of the places I had visited.) As usual, I went three days ahead of the scheduled event to work with the media. I was also to help some local school children build a special wreath made of flowers, for this particular exhibit was designed to emphasize the children who were on the *Titanic*.

The day of the event began with a parade down the Atlantic City Boardwalk. I rode on a float, along with some children holding the large flowered wreath, all the while standing and giving the traditional Miss America wave, as a recording played Celine Dion singing "My Heart Will Go On."

The parade ended at the casino, where a stage had been built outside for this special event. There was a string quartet playing ragtime music that, no doubt, had also been played on the *Titanic*. My job was to go up on that stage, give the captain's last speech and talk about how many children were on the *Titanic* and what happened to them. When I had finished, I was to take the wreath and two children with me and walk slowly down to the waterfront, as the names of all the children who died that day were read. This was to be a very sacred and dignified moment, and it was... until we arrived at the waterfront.

My instructions were to get into a lifeboat with the wreath, along with two lifeguards, and let them row me out past the breakers. Then I was to stand up and throw the wreath into the water. At that moment, the whistle was to sound, and then the string quartet was to play "Nearer My God to Thee." This would have been very moving, but, as you already know, things don't always work right on the *Titanic*.

For some reason, I had a strong feeling of apprehension about getting into that lifeboat, not because I was afraid of the water or the boat, but because I was wearing a new uniform for the first time. Not only was it expensive, but it had been custom-made for me, and I didn't want to get it soiled by sitting in an old boat. But, like a good seaman, I did what I was told, saying goodbye to the children and stepping gingerly into the lifeboat. We shoved off, and the two lifeguards began to row.

As we pulled out from shore, one of the lifeguards said, "Captain, the breakers are very large today. I don't think we're going to have enough time to make it out past them, so I think you need to throw the wreath somewhere in between."

I thought to myself, "You've got to be kidding!"

The sea was very rough that day, but I did my best. I decided to wait for a large breaker to roll under us, and then I stood up and threw the wreath into the water.

At that moment, it felt like a tsunami hit our boat! The front of the boat went high into the air and then took a nosedive back into the water. This automatically threw the back end even higher, propelling me like a slingshot into the air. I was totally airborne, flipping back so that both of my feet were higher than my head. We've all heard it said that if you're in a life-threatening situation, your whole life flashes before you. Mine didn't. I didn't think about God or my wife. All I could think was "DON'T FALL INTO THE WATER!" I didn't want to get my new uniform wet.

Fortunately (or unfortunately), I landed on my back in the boat, just in time to see a huge breaker come over the top of us, drenching us all. It was a miracle I wasn't injured, but my new uniform and my dignity did suffer some damage. Sometimes, the smallest decision can change your entire future and the paths of countless others as well. That was certainly true for Captain Smith and for all the others connected with the *Titanic*.

CHAPTER 5

TEN-CENT DESTINY

World War II continued to rage throughout my elementary years, and although I was just a child, I was very aware of the many boys in our community who didn't make it back. The war had a great impact on every man, woman, and child, and as I left elementary school and prepared to move on to middle school, the war continued to create a sense of urgency and duty in me, as it did in everyone else.

Terry was now eighteen, graduating from high school and preparing to go to college at Moody Bible Institute in Chicago to become a preacher. Somehow, over the years, he had grown to become a great encouragement and help to his scrawny little brother, and I had grown to look up to and admire him. So Terry was off to Bible school as I was entering adolescence; I had no thoughts about what I would be doing when it became my turn to graduate from high school.

In the summer of 1945, as my first years of middle school were just beginning, I heard on the radio that the war was over. I got a spoon and a large pan from our kitchen, put it in the basket of Terry's Silver King bicycle, and rode up and down the street banging that pan with the spoon and shouting, "The war is over! The war is over!" I think I even waved to Old Lady Powell. That evening, Michigan Avenue downtown was jammed with people, all shouting and yelling. We were so glad that the boys were finally coming home!

I began this next chapter of my life at West Intermediate School. I had to say goodbye to Harley because he went to a different school, so I was on my own now. Like everyone entering middle school for the first time, I was intimidated. This was a big place, no longer a one-room schoolhouse with the windows open all of the time.

By the time I reached the eighth grade, I wanted to play the trumpet in the band. Mr. Shoemaker, the music director, looked at me and said, "Close your mouth and let me see your teeth." After a short glance, he said, "Trombone," and that was that. I learned to play the trombone well. This small decision, made by my band director, would not fall outside of God's plan, but would become something He would use in my life over and over to put me where He wanted me to be. When things happened to me outside of my own control, I learned not to think for a moment that God would not make good use of it. He would!

Christmas time rolled around again, and Dad said, "Here is a Johnson Smith catalog. You boys should circle anything you want for Christmas, up to five dollars." Johnson Smith & Company was located in Detroit, and their catalog was full of everything a teen could imagine wanting. I circled $4.90 worth of items, but I wasn't about to settle for $4.90. I was bound and determined to spend the other ten cents. I went back and forth through that little catalog and finally found an item for ten cents. It was a little booklet entitled *How to Become a Ventriloquist*, and it was by Edgar Bergen, a famous ventriloquist in his own right.

That little ten-cent decision became another pivotal moment in my life, starting me on a career that would present me with my first great crossroad and eventually pay for my college education. In time, my ventriloquism was a talent that God would use to reach thousands for

Him. We must never doubt God's guiding hand in every situation, even every obstacle. He will surely use every little ten-cent decision we ever make.

I studied that booklet for about a year, and when the word got out that I had learned ventriloquism, Ganson Street Baptist Church contacted me and wanted me to perform my routine at their daily Vacation Bible School. I had several months to prepare for the occasion, but there were two things wrong: (1) I had no dummy, and (2) I had no routine.

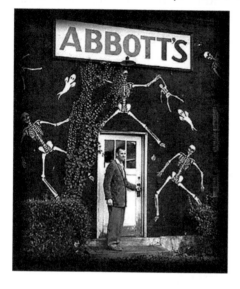

Abbott's Magic Novelty Company[6] opened in 1934 in Colon, Michigan, and is still one of the best sources for magic tricks, supplies, and instructions in the world. I wrote to Abbott's for a ventriloquist script and "patter" (a term that just means the back and forth conversation between the dummy and the ventriloquist). In the meantime, Terry came up with an idea for how to make a dummy out of a coconut. We painted a face on a coconut, cut open a mouth and hooked it up with a rubber band and a string with a ring on the end, so that I could pull it up and down. Then we drilled a half-inch hole where the neck would be. We placed a bolt about eight inches long in the opening, along with two nuts, one on the inside of the coconut head and the other on the outside, and tightened them both up, so I could use that bolt to hold on to and turn the dummy's head.

Now we needed something to use for a body. We found a cigar box, covered it with a jacket and used that as a torso, hung some home-made stuffed arms and legs on it, and, *voila!* "Henry" was born.

All I needed now was the routine, which didn't arrive until the day before the program. To my surprise, all the material I received was blue, meaning it had been written for an adult nightclub audience, not the best choice for Vacation Bible School. What was I going to do?

The day came, and I stood on the platform at Ganson Street Baptist Church in front of five hundred children, about to tell the only clean story that Abbott's had sent me. The dummy was to do all the talking. It went like this:

HENRY: A mother sent her little son to the store to get a bottle of milk. She gave him ten cents and an empty milk bottle. On the way, the boy dropped the bottle and broke it. He went home and said, "I'm sorry, Mama, I dropped the bottle and broke it."

She said, "I'll give you another bottle, but be more careful this time."

He took the bottle and started off to the store, but now he accidentally dropped the dime. He went back home and said, "Mama, I'm sorry, but I lost the dime."

She said, "I'll give you another dime, but come back with the milk this time, or I'll KILL YOU!"

So, off he went to the store, and on the way he dropped the bottle and lost the dime."

(I waited for Henry to continue, but he also just waited.)

LOWELL: (Feigning frustration) SO WHAT HAPPENED? (Again Henry paused dramatically and then concluded.)

HENRY : She KILLED him!

The children were stunned, and I heard nothing, no response whatsoever from them. You could hear crickets chirping, and I died a horrible death. There had been no Christian message and no spiritual application, and now there was no response except silence.

Could it get any worse? Yes. In the process of telling the story, I had turned the bolt so many times that it loosened the nuts, and when I turned and started to walk off of the platform, Henry's head fell off and split into pieces right in front of the kids. The first two rows of children started to cry. I was never invited back to that church.

As an eighth grader, I struggled like everyone else with very low self-esteem, always self-conscious about my thin frame. I was willing to try anything to be identified by something other than being skinny. My first shot at ventriloquism, however, had not helped my insecurities at all. I would need more practice, and I kept looking for some magic combination of talents.

When Terry came home from Chicago for Christmas vacation that year, he brought along some magic tricks he had purchased there, and being the entrepreneur that he was, he sold them to me at a profit. I was happy to pay. This was the combination I thought I needed to escape from my debilitating insecurities: magic and ventriloquism combined. It would be perfect! I practiced and practiced, and once again I was invited to do a show at a church on the north end of town, this time a magic show.

The program was to take place in the basement of the church right after the main service. Cliff Barrows was there, leading the song service with his trombone, the man who would become so well-known within the Billy Graham organization. After the main service had ended, Cliff invited the congregation to go down to the basement and see the young magician.

I was trying out a new trick that I had just bought that day. It seemed to be a simple trick and easy to do, involving pouring milk into a man's borrowed hat. A trusting audience member became my willing participant. With his hat in my left hand, the pitcher of milk in my right, I actually poured milk into his very expensive Stetson hat. Everyone in the audience thought it was all part of the act... until the bottom of the hat started to turn dark and milk began to run down my arm. I was just a kid, with no well-rehearsed ad-libs, so I just said, "I goofed," and then I turned around and went into the kitchen, feeling extremely embarrassed.

Afterward, I offered to pay for the hat, but the man said, "Forget it. It was worth the laugh."

I thought to myself, "I hope I never see that man again," but ten years later, I was playing my trombone in a church service in Detroit. After the service, a man came to me and said, "Do you remember pouring milk into my hat?" Even though my magic skills had improved greatly by that point, my old insecurities instantly came bouncing back.

With one of my character dummies at a show

I continued to practice my magic tricks and ventriloquism throughout my intermediate school years, putting on shows for the neighborhood kids. Always the entrepreneur, I charged ten cents for a one-hour show. Over those critical years, I became very accustomed to receiving applause and the attention performance brought, and I became less and less insecure, the more I performed.

In high school, I found a new opportunity to satisfy my hunger for attention, this time through drama. One particular performance in my freshman year catapulted me from being insecure to being self-confident at the expense of everything else. I performed a monologue written by Leota Hulse Black called "Scratch, the Newsboy's Dog." By the end of the performance, there was hardly a dry eye in the house. I was given a standing ovation, and my sense that I might be worth something after all was reinforced when the students congratulated me over and over again throughout the week. As with most young people in that stage of life, everything in my world revolved around me—my insecurities, my talents, my life.

CHAPTER 6

DUMMY

I danced precariously close to the less wholesome side of entertainment, performing and perfecting my act in local restaurants, bars, and nightclubs at night, even as I continued to perform for churches, schools, and other Christian audiences during the day. I invested heavily in the act, buying more and more magic tricks and creating new characters with more dummies.

My ego continued to rise, and my need to rely on God and serve Him began to diminish with every success, every round of applause, every new opportunity. Through it all, my mother prayed for me, concerned about the direction I was headed, entrusting me to God's wisdom and control. There were many times during those years when God intervened, protecting me from the many tragedies and accidents that often befall young people, the consequences of rash decisions or blindly getting into dangerous situations. Like the *Titanic*, I was speeding quickly away from a healthy walk with God and into a path strewn with the dangerous icebergs of pride, money, success, ego, and fame.

During my senior year in high school, one of my classmates said to me, "Lowell, the *Horace Heidt Show* is coming to town. You ought to try out for it."

The *Horace Heidt Show* was a talent contest that was broadcast on radio nationwide, the most popular show of its kind. It was credited with giving a start to such iconic celebrities as Johnny Carson, Art Carney, the King Sisters, Gordon McCrae, and many others. Elvis Presley tried to audition, but was turned away because he hadn't brought a copy of his songs with him.

Program from the Horace Heidt Show

I went down to the Municipal Auditorium in Jackson, where the audition was to take place, and found more than five hundred people waiting to try out. When my turn came, they asked me what I was going to do. I said, "I am a ventriloquist."

They asked, "Do you have a copy of your routine?"

"No," I answered, "I just ad-lib it." I never did have a firm routine written down. Unlike Elvis, for some reason, they let me audition anyway.

Finally, the big day came. Horace Heidt and his big band, the Musical Knights, arrived in Jackson. The auditorium was packed. Dick Contino, the famous accordion player, was there. He would shake his accordion bellows when he played "Lady of Spain," and videos can still be found online of his amazing performances.

When Horace Heidt introduced me that night, he called me Lowell Lytellie. He never could get my name right. I was shaking like a leaf. I had made the big time.

The radio show was sponsored by Philip Morris cigarettes, and their spokesperson was Johnny Roventini. Only forty-seven inches tall, Johnny dressed like a bell hop and would deliver his famous line at the end of every show as the band played "The Donkey Serenade" behind him: "Call for Philip Morris! C-a-l-l for Philip M-o-r-r-i-s-!" In the heat of the moment, I decided to let my dummy use Roventini's words to end my three-minute act, and it went like this:

Poster of Johnny Roventiti

HENRY: This is Johnny again, folks, returning to thousands of store windows all over America. Look for me. I'll be waiting for you. Come in and... call for Philip Morris, c-a-l-l for Philip M-o-r-r-i-s!

The band picked up the cue and played "The Donkey Serenade" while Henry was saying all of this. At the end, the band hit a big chord, and I jumped up and ran off the stage.

The audience loved it, and I won the *Horace Heidt Show*. What an experience for a 17-year-old! My parents were there that night, along with my brother Terry and his wife, Olive. After all the congratulations, the night came to an end, and I finally went to bed around midnight. Mom, who had been praying for me all my life, knew that I was at a serious crossroads. After the success of the show that night, she could see that I was getting dangerously close to a lifestyle far removed from my Christian values. Late into the night, she came up to my room, knelt down beside my bed, and prayed. I am sure she prayed for both Terry and me on many sleepless nights over the years. Who knows how many times it was those prayers that spared us much grief? My eyes were closed that night, but I was awake and could hear her soft whispers, her fervent plea: "Lord, get a hold of my boy. With all his talent, let him use it for Your glory."

Up until that point, ventriloquism had been a major part of my blossoming career. When I would reach down in my suitcase and pick up Henry, he was lifeless and had nothing to contribute to society. But when I placed him on my lap, pulled a few strings, and gave him a voice, within ten seconds the audience would feel that he was alive. In fact, for me to be able to interact with Henry, I had to treat him as if he really were alive from the moment I sat him on my lap. Henry could say things I might not have the courage to say, and the audience would listen to him. Through Henry, I received fame, the promise of riches, an identity, a sense of accomplishment, and self-worth.

Through Henry, I learned to overcome my deep insecurities and found a niche that was far away from the shadow cast by my big brother, of whom I knew my parents were very proud. Now I was on the verge of something huge; this felt like the greatest night of my life, and held for me the biggest promise of all. Yet, here was my mother, who had led me to Christ, who had disciplined me and done everything she could to help me succeed and feel loved and accepted, who had nurtured my creativity and musical gifts and given me the freedom as a child to find my own unique path, and she was kneeling at my bedside praying for what? Did she want me to give it all up? I had been playing in night clubs already, and surely my success with the *Horace Heidt Show* would lead me further down that path. How could I use my talent for God's glory there?

After Mom left the room, I lay there for about an hour contemplating what the Lord would want me to do. Mom's words, spoken to me night after night as a child, came back to me: "Look out there at the sky. Those clouds could open up any minute. Listen for a trumpet to sound, for the Lord could come back at any time. You see those lights in the houses out there? Those people don't know about Jesus, and it's up to us to tell them."

I thought about the plaque that was hanging in our living room that said, "Only one life, twill soon be past. Only what's done for Christ will last." About three o'clock in the morning, I got out of bed, opened up my magic prop suitcases, took out all the magic tricks, and scattered them all over the room, along with my three dummies. I got down on my knees and prayed: "God, if all of this can be used for You, so be it. If not, that will be just fine too. But I'm going to put You first in my life."

The next day I went down to the local newspaper and told the reporters that I would not be pursuing a career in entertainment. Instead, when I graduated from high school, I would be attending Moody Bible Institute and going into the ministry. Since I had just won the *Horace Heidt Show*, I'm sure there were many people upset with me because of this decision, but my vision had to be vertical, not horizontal.

That fall, I kept my promise and was on my way to Chicago to begin Bible college. I walked away from what I felt was a certain and very bright future. Some people imagine that the Christian life is boring and limited, so they seek the opportunities the secular world has to offer. I had no idea of the jaw-dropping adventures that awaited me because of my decision, a life full beyond measure, far different, more powerful, and more fulfilling by a great distance than the life I had walked away from. I had no idea then how many thousands of other lives would be affected by that fervent prayer of my faithful mother.

Now, I was in college, at the very school my brother had attended. I had brought my overconfidence, enormous ego, and brash enthusiasm with me, yet all those old insecurities were still simmering just beneath the surface. God had a lot of work to do to shape my weaknesses into my strengths, beginning with a good dose of humility. Slowly, something was beginning to be transformed within me, a change that would not be complete until... well, even now. Well over sixty years later, God is still working on me.

What was the transformation? In my youth, I had learned how to control my dummy, how to sit him on my lap and get him to do whatever I wanted. Henry never fought back, never resisted, but always sat comfortably on my lap and allowed me to control him. He never argued about the places we would perform and never failed to show up. Still, he had a way of speaking to me. What would Henry teach me? And who was controlling whom? I had so much to learn.

With Regis Philbin on the Grand Staircase, Branson Titanic Museum

CAPTAIN'S LOG: PHILBIN'S FOLLY
Dateline: Summer 2006 - BRANSON, MISSOURI

Branson, Missouri, and Pigeon Forge, Tennessee, have two of the largest *Titanic* attractions in the world. Mary Kellogg and her husband, John Joslyn, have actually rebuilt the *Titanic* at half scale in each city. You can hardly believe it. You'll be driving down the road, and then suddenly a huge ship comes into view and looks like it's crossing the road in front of you. The model stands a hundred feet tall, and water is splashing on the bow. What an amazing sight it is!

Certain parts of the interior of the ship were reproduced full scale, for example, the grand staircase, and the first- and third-class berths. It's quite an experience to visit one of these exhibits, and if you ever travel to one of these two cities, make sure your itinerary includes a visit to the *Titanic*. Each museum has a wonderful crew of actors and actresses to give you a tour you will never forget. When they built each ship, they gave me the honor of christening them. The first to be christened was in Branson. Regis Philbin would be there to emcee the event, along with the mayor of the city, two of Molly Brown's great granddaughters—Muffet Brown and Helen Benziger—and the owners of the attraction.

The big day arrived. They had built a stage down by the front of the ship, where all the special guests would give their remarks. I was to be on the bow of the ship, along with three other officers, a hundred feet above the crowd and hidden out of sight for the first part of the program.

When Regis introduced us, the four of us were to suddenly step up into the view of the crowd, building excitement and anticipation for the big finale. I was supposed to take a champagne bottle, put it in a bag, tie a rope around the bag,

The crew of the Titanic Museum on the Grand Staircase, Branson, Missouri - 2017

and at the right moment, fling it over the bow, smashing it against the ship. Just then, rockets would be fired from the deck, and the band would play. It all sounded easy enough, and we practiced the entire scene the day before. I suggested to the owners that they get one of those precut champagne bottles that are easy to break. We've all seen people christen a ship, only to see the bottle bounce off and not break. I preferred not to be a part of that!

"In fact," I added, "you might want to get two of them, just in case one of them breaks prematurely." They agreed and bought two bottles. But, as you will remember, things don't always work right on the *Titanic*! In order to get on deck, we had to be lifted up by a crane, as there was no access to the deck from the inside of the ship. We came in from the back side so nobody would see us. On the forward part of the deck, somebody had built a small elevated platform and placed four chairs and four water bottles near them. And that was it. There was nothing else on the deck except for two men who were stationed about fifty feet from us, preparing rockets to send up after the christening. I really didn't pay much attention to them.

The only thing I carried with me was a small styrofoam box containing one of the precut champagne bottles wrapped in bubble wrap. "Oh, by the way," I was told, as I took possession of the box, "one of the bottles has already broken, so this is it. Be careful with it!"

I sat down, along with the other men, my styrofoam box in hand, while waiting for the program to begin. Of course, I was already miked for sound, but the organizers also gave me a headset, so that I could hear when I was to be introduced from down below. It appeared to me that there were more than a thousand people in attendance, along with a band that was down in front just behind the television camera.

When the program started, I very carefully opened the lid of the styrofoam box, unwrapped the bubble wrap, and gently removed the champagne bottle. I stood to my feet, to make sure I was ready when Regis introduced me. Thirty minutes later, they were still giving opening speeches, and I got a little tired standing there with the bottle, so I thought to myself, "I'll just gently set this down on the platform and wait for them to finish." I gingerly set the bottle down, but it was so fragile that the bottom of it broke anyway, and all of the liquid spilled out! "OH, NO!" I thought to myself, "THIS CAN'T BE HAPPENING! I'VE JUST RUINED THE CHRISTENING!"

Helping Regis Philbin stoke the Titanic museum's furnace with coal

The Joslyn's were down below on stage, waiting with anticipation for the moment that I would climb up on the platform, along with the three officers, make a short speech, and then fling the bottle over the side, smashing it against the bow. BUT, NO! NOW THERE WAS NO CHAMPAGNE! THERE WAS NO BOTTLE! THERE WAS NOTHING! My heart sank, and I remember all the blood in my body rushing to my head, making it difficult for me to think of what to do next.

I had to do something. I had to make it happen, but how? Time was running out. All of the speakers were finished with their speeches, except for Regis, who was just about to introduce me.

I turned what was left of the bottle upside down and asked one of the officers to pour some water into it. He did this, but the water just ran out of the neck of the bottle. So that didn't work!

I looked around for anything that might work. Somebody had left a champagne glass next to the main mast. I grabbed the glass and had a crew member pour water into it, thinking that maybe I could put that in the bag, and with centrifugal force, keep the water in the glass until it hit the side of the ship. Then I said to the officers, "Do you see any duct tape around here?" What a dumb question! There was nothing up there except for four chairs and four plastic bottles of water.

But, "Wait a minute!" I said. As I looked over to the men who were preparing to launch the rockets, I saw a small roll of duct tape. I had one of the officers quickly go over and get it, so that we could try to tape over the top of the glass, holding the water in place. When I was a kid, if you wanted to fix something in an emergency, the only thing you had was bailing wire. Well, duct tape is the bailing wire of the twenty-first century. The only problem with duct tape is that it will not stick to something wet, and by now, water had splashed all over the glass. We did our best, hoping that some of it would stick, but of course it didn't. We jammed as much of the glass as we could into a bag and tied the end of the rope to it, just as I heard on my earphones Regis asking, "Is there a captain on board?"

That was our cue to start walking up the steps. I was told later that it really was a "WOW" effect to see all four officers on the deck appear out of nowhere. No one below could see that I was shaking like a leaf. I didn't want to disappoint Mary and John.

I was afraid that none of this would work and we would all be embarrassed, but I had to give it my best effort. I answered, "Yes, Regis, and I would like to..." At that moment, the clock struck twelve, and an automatic timer turned on two large horns that had been placed on the deck to go off every day just at that time, and they were aimed right at me. The volume those two horns produced was overpowering, for they were designed to replicate the sound of a large ship. They were so loud that I could hardly think of what I had just said.

There were three long blasts with a few seconds in between. Regis, being the professional that he is, tried to fill the dead space with comments like, "What's the matter with the captain? Get the captain off the ship!" I just stood there freaking out.

Finally, the horns stopped blasting, and I recovered enough to say, "I would like to christen the *Titanic* for a smooth sail in the city of Branson, Missouri." With that, I grabbed the end of the rope, said a prayer under my breath, and then swung the glass in a large arc over the side of the ship.

The water started to spurt out in all directions, and some of it hit Regis. Some of it hit the television cameras, and some hit a trombone player in the first row of the band. I had no idea whether any of it hit the side of the ship. At this point, my mind was blown. I didn't even hear the rockets go up. I was told later that it had all gone off "very well."

Christening the Titanic Museum in Branson

CHAPTER 7

JAILHOUSE JAM

True to my word, the summer after high school I prepared to begin my studies at Moody Bible Institute in Chicago, just as my brother Terry had done before being called to serve as pastor of a little church in Devils Lake, Michigan, and that fall I traveled to Chicago to begin my studies. One of the first things I did at Moody was to form an evangelistic team comprised of a trombone trio and a speaker by the name of Millard Saul.

Not surprisingly, my somewhat rebellious and risk-taking nature didn't fit well with the restrictions an ultra-conservative Bible college such as Moody placed on me, and although I was an average student learning the material, like many college freshmen, I spent too much time socializing and staying up late, eventually looking for an opportunity to follow my passion for evangelism by a different path.

Terry had been using his own creative gifts to find new ways to reach people for Christ. If people would not come to church to hear the Gospel, perhaps they would come to a drive-in with their cars and listen to the message. The first commercial drive-in theater had been built back in 1933, and by 1950, drive-in theaters were wildly popular, allowing people to see a movie without having to dress up, find a baby-sitter, or even leave the comfort of their car. Terry was one of a growing number of pastors who realized this concept might be a good way to spread the Gospel.

While I was in school in Chicago, Terry built a little platform at Devils Lake in the middle of a cornfield for his first drive-in church. The little building was sixteen feet wide, eight feet deep, and eight feet tall, with room for storage and equipment underneath, and just enough room on the roof to put a piano. Loudspeakers were attached to each side of the building.

When I decided to leave Moody, I called Terry and asked him if he could use our evangelistic team at his church that next summer. As it turned out, our first program in Devils Lake was also the first program at the drive-in church. The place was packed that night. "Wow!" I thought. "Maybe Terry is onto something!"

The only problem seemed to be the location. It was right next to a swamp, and you can imagine how many bugs would be floating around in the night air. I remember my father standing under the platform with a bug bomb, reaching up and spraying the flood lights, where all the mosquitoes seemed to gather. I'd be up on the platform trying to play my trombone, and with each breath, I'd be siphoning mosquitoes through my teeth—no easy task. When it came time for our speaker, he handled the situation quite well... until he swallowed a bug. After hacking and coughing for about a minute, he said, "At least I was scriptural. 'He was a stranger, and I took him in.'"

That same summer, Mom found an advertisement for a Christian college in beautiful Clearwater, Florida, where Billy Graham had attended. If Moody wasn't the right fit for my training, maybe this would be the place. My high school pal Bruce Duddles went with me, and we arrived in Clearwater in mid-November in my 1947 Studebaker coup. We couldn't believe how warm it was. The grass was green, there were palm trees, and the flowers were blooming. Why in the world had we been living in Michigan all these years?

With Bruce on our Road Trip

I got a few odd jobs to support myself, still trying to be obedient to my commitment to use my gifts and talents for God, but all my work together was not enough. Eventually, I decided to sell my beloved car to cover my school costs, but within two days of placing the ad to sell it, a school official accidentally backed into it, crushing the side door—and he didn't take responsibility for the damages. Frustrated and disillusioned, I called Bruce, and we agreed to take our last dollars, fill the gas tank, and head south to beautiful Miami, two young men on the expedition of a lifetime.

Late on our first night driving through the central part of Florida, I could see the lights of a little town ahead called Avon Park. I was driving about sixty miles an hour when I came upon a sign that said "25 MPH." I took my foot off the gas and began to slow down, but it was too late. I saw the flashing lights of a police car in my rearview mirror. It was a speed trap.

The officer said I would have to pay a $25 fine in cash because I was from out of state. "It took all of our money to fill up the gas tank," I told him. "I'm sorry, but I don't have $25." Bruce didn't say anything.

"Do you have any friends down here or someone who could wire you the money?" he asked. "If not, you'll have to go to jail."

I didn't relish the idea, but we had no place to sleep that night anyway, so I said, "Then, I guess we'll have to go to jail." We meant me, since I was the driver being fined. Bruce made plans to sleep out front of the jail in the Studebaker with all of our gear.

Much like the fictional town of Mayberry, protected by the beloved Andy Taylor, Avon Park had its own equally affable jail keeper who watched over a tiny three-cell jailhouse. It was very cold that night, and there was no heat and no blankets in those bare cells. It was also very cold out in the Studebaker, so Duddles asked if he could join me, and I asked if he could bring in our suitcases, with blankets and pillows inside. "Of course!" the jailer agreed. We hunkered down for a long night.

After a while, being a little bored, I asked the jail keeper if we could go out and get my trombone and Bruce's clarinet. "Sure!" he said, his eyes lighting up. "In fact, I've got a bass up in the attic. I'll go get it, and we can jam!" He never did grab his bass, but some firemen from a firehouse attached to the jail heard us playing and brought their own instruments in to join us. We held our own private jailhouse jam that lasted for several hours! It turned out to be a pretty good night after all.

The next morning, the jailer was unprepared to feed us, so someone was sent to bring us bacon and eggs from a restaurant across the street, and another great meal for lunch. Bruce and I looked at each other and said, "This is a pretty good deal. We should stay here a few more days!" A short time later, however, a police officer came in and said, "We can't afford to feed you guys. Come up with the money, or we'll have to put you on the chain gang."

During the 1950s, chain gangs were still used in Florida to punish prisoners and get work done that no one else wanted to do. We didn't know if he was serious or not, but that's all that Bruce needed to hear. He opened his suitcase, ripped open the lining, and pulled out a $20 bill he had hidden there for an emergency. They settled for that, and before we knew it, we were on our way. My family and I drove through that town thirty years later and stopped in the old jailhouse, sharing our incredible story with the officer at the front desk. "Yes, you're right," he laughed. "Thirty years ago, that stretch of road was a speed trap."

The day after our close encounter with a chain gang, Bruce and I made it to Miami, immediately fell asleep on the beach, and woke up a few hours later badly sunburned. "Oh yeah," I thought, "this is going to be fun." But the only place we had to sleep was in the car, and it had mohair seats. I was in the back seat and Bruce was in the front, but my long legs were dangling over the steering wheel and getting in his way. Every time we turned, our sunburned skin would scrape against those mohair seats. We were so miserable that we barely spoke to each other for days.

Back then, it was permitted to pick up oranges that had fallen from the trees in the orange groves. We lived on oranges for the next week, after which we both had a mouthful of canker sores. This couldn't continue. We had to find work somewhere.

I followed an ad in the Miami Herald and got a job about twenty-five miles north in Lake Worth, working as a houseman, and Bruce found a job as a busboy. I had no idea what a houseman's job entailed, but it turned out that I was to stay in one of the four servants' quarters on the mansion's property. The first night in that place, I was lying in bed reading my Bible, when suddenly I looked up and saw a huge spider on the beam above my head. It was at least six inches long. I put down my Bible and picked up a *Life* magazine. I rolled it up, slowly stood to my feet, cocked my arm back, and started to swing at that ugly, hairy thing. Instantly, it vanished into the side walls of my cabin. Oh, great!

There were a lot of spiders in that room, and for the most part, spiders didn't bother me, but there was something about living with that large spider that I didn't like. Worse, the next morning I woke up with spider bites on one arm. That was enough for me. The next day, Bruce and I headed back north to Michigan.

I imagine my mother was praying hard for me during all this time, as I had once again begun to veer off course. Were speeding tickets, spiders, and sunburns perhaps the result of a mother's prayers? Later, despite everything, God would use this detour in a powerful way. I would find myself returning to Florida sooner than I imagined.

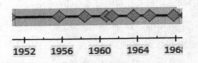

1952   1956   1960   1964   196?

SETTING THE SAILS

The most deceiving part about playing the role of Captain Smith, such a dignified gentleman, is that inside and behind the scenes sometimes I'm just a big dummy like Henry, a dummy who's jumped off of the lap of God, and it seems that no one is in control.

For many of us, this is particularly true during our precarious twenties and thirties, when we are so sure of ourselves, confident we know everything about the world, and yet to experience our first major setback.

We are building our lives, following our dreams, forging ahead on pure adrenaline and determination. We set the sails into the wind and think we are headed toward our final destination, our perfect future. It's not until much later that we realize we were just getting started, still learning to read the wind and the sky, testing the limits of the ship.

So began my first dive into the deep. I had no idea it would not be my last.

CHAPTER 8

NUMBER 87

After I had gotten out of high school, with my overconfidence and inflated ego in full swing, I had set a personal goal of dating at least ninety-nine girls before I got married. I just wanted to make sure I got the right one. Imagine going on a date with someone who not only started talking about marriage right away, but also let you know what number you were in his search for "Ms. Right!" I would actually hand each girl a little paper heart with a number on it and say, "Keep this number, and when I get to #99, I might call you." I can't imagine what the girls must have thought of that. How arrogant can one person be? Somehow, I just thought it was fun.

I had decided to stay in Michigan to complete my education at the Grand Rapids School of the Bible and Music, and was working and saving money to pay for my tuition during the summer, while I helped Terry at Devils Lake on the drive-in project. Of course, I also continued to work on my ninety-nine dates.

Through multiple attempts at building a screen that could be used to show Billy Graham films and other Christian productions, we worked extra jobs to support ourselves and pay for materials and designed and built every attempt at a screen, improving the property, adding parking, and doing anything we could to draw people in. The fruit of the seeds planted in designing and building all of those projects together in our youth was coming back to us.

The first attempt at a screen was made out of 2x4s, and that winter it blew down. The second attempt also was blown down just a few months after it went up. For the third attempt the following year, we used utility poles to support the screen, and that one stood for years to come.

With Terry and the model of the Devils Lake Drive-in

For the next three years, I studied in Bible college throughout the school year and then spent the summer at Devils Lake, working with Terry on the drive-in program. I also continued singing, playing trombone, and finding opportunities to perform my magic tricks and ventriloquism in ways that I thought would have a spiritual application or be of service to God in some way.

Each summer, about sixteen thousand tourists would come out to Devils Lake on any given weekend, but only some fifty faithful

The completed Devils Lake Drive-in

people were regularly attending Terry's church there. So he and I put a generator in the back of his station wagon and speakers on top, and we would drive all around the town on Saturday and Sunday, inviting people to come to the drive-in. This seemed to work. We actually packed the place out.

During my last year in college, I almost achieved my goal of ninety-nine dates. Number 87 was a charming little gal named Barbara.

Barbara was kind, gentle, talented, and a strong Christian. She had the loveliest smile and sparkling eyes. Oh, and did I mention how pretty she was? And Barbara was also very smart. In fact, she was the teacher in one of my music classes.

Barbara wasn't quite as taken with me. "I didn't see what all the girls saw in him," she said. "He was so full of himself! Privately, he was okay as a person, and he actually was handsome. We became good friends, but only friends. It could never turn into anything else!" Barbara was not interested in me, and I was still twelve dates short of my goal, so I had to keep looking.

*The heart I gave Barbara
on our first date*

I was discussing marriage with #92, when she said, "You keep talking about this girl, Barbara. I think you're in love with her." I started thinking about that and decided that she was right. I was in love with Barbara, and so I didn't need to look any further.

Thank God, Barbara wasn't too put off by my methodical approach to finding the perfect mate. I somehow managed to sway her opinion of me, and we began dating in earnest. After everything it took for us to get together, I still was in no hurry. We had been good friends for many years and then dated each other exclusively for almost a year, but I felt I needed one more sign from God that she was the one for me.

Barb suffered a lot from her reproductive system, and this sometimes required a hospital stay. I was selling Filter Queen vacuum cleaners at the time, while still in school, tough work that never resulted in more than two or three sales a week. I visited Barb in the hospital one afternoon before work. We had recently talked about marriage "sometime in the next four or five years." I said to her that day, "If I sell two vacuum cleaners tonight, we'll set the date." I figured this was a pretty safe bet, for I had never sold two in one night. That night, however, to my surprise, I did it! That's what love will do. After my second sale, I headed for the hospital. We made it official and set the date.

That Christmas, I gave Barbara a large paper heart that had "100" on it. It is kept in a special keepsake box to this day. I guess those paper hearts were not such a bad idea after all.

Throughout the years, as we shared this story, I would always say, "We've been married all these years, and I'm still in love with #87."

With Barbara, cutting the wedding cake

Barbara and I were married in Ionia, Michigan, her hometown, on June 3, 1955, and after I graduated we spent the next winter working in Lansing, Michigan, for an organization called Youth for Christ.

The next summer, we were back at the drive-in, which, of course, could only operate during warmer weather. Barb's doctor had told her that she would probably never have any children, so we bought a house trailer with just one bedroom and a long living room, where she could have her piano, and parked the trailer right behind the drive-in screen.

During our early years together, I did whatever I could to earn money. Whether it was selling vacuum cleaners or doing landscaping, everything I did in some way taught me skills I would rely on in the years ahead.

The crew of the Titanic Museum on the Grand Staircase, Pigeon Forge, Tennessee - 2017

CAPTAIN'S LOG: THE REVIVAL OF CAPTAIN SMITH

Dateline: Summer 2002-2013 - VARIOUS UNITED STATES TOURS

While I'm working at the *Titanic* exhibits, I meet people from all walks of life. Some of my time is spent walking through the exhibit, telling stories and describing the artifacts, but most of my time is spent standing in front of a large picture of the Grand Staircase, having my picture taken with hundreds of people before they go into the exhibit.

One day, a man in his fifties came out of the exhibit and was standing about seventy-five feet from me in the parking lot with the curator. He pointed his finger at me and said in all sincerity, "That man should be ashamed of himself! He killed all those people, and now he's standing there getting his picture taken and making money at it! Shame on him!" I guess it meant that I was pretty convincing as the captain. I can't say what it meant about that poor soul.

Many years ago, there was a television program called *Kids Say the Darndest Things*, and it's true. I was in Chicago at the Museum of Science and Industry, working at the *Titanic* exhibition there, and a lady came up to me with her 7-year-old boy. "My son knows everything about the *Titanic*," she said, "and he would like to have his picture taken with you." I'm always intrigued when I see young people who are that interested in the *Titanic*.

It seems like every time I'm interviewed on the media, the first question I'm asked is: "After all these years, why are so many people still interested in the *Titanic*?" I wish I had a good answer to that question. What I can say is that the *Titanic* was the largest man-made moving object ever built and the most luxurious ship of its time. It was carrying some of the wealthiest

Answering questions for museum visitors

people in the world, and at the same time, some of the poorest. It was supposedly unsinkable, and yet when it collided with an iceberg on its maiden voyage, it took only two hours and forty minutes to sink. That time lapse allowed many of the people involved to think about their destiny. You couldn't make up a story like that, and many people are still writing about it. In fact, it's the third most written about event in history.

I thought to myself, "Maybe this 7-year-old boy has the answer," so I sat him down after we took the photo and asked, "Why are you so interested in the *Titanic* at your age?"

He looked up into the air and thought about it, and then answered, "Well, I like beautiful things, and I like to break things." That sounded like a 7-year-old to me.

I usually split my time portraying the captain between the permanent exhibits at Branson and Pigeon Forge, where fine crews make sure every visitor to the museum has a wonderful experience. I was in Pigeon Forge when a little girl and her parents came up to me. The mother said, "Our daughter is very interested in the *Titanic*."

I bent over and said, "So, you like the *Titanic*?"

"Yes, very much so!" "What is your name?" "My name is Sarah."

We talked for a few minutes about the *Titanic*, and as we spoke I couldn't help but notice that she was exceptionally brilliant. "How old are you?" I asked.

"Seven."

"You remind me of my grandson, Steven," I told her. "He's also seven, and he's sharp, just like you!"

We talked a little more about the *Titanic*, and I gave her my business card. She turned and started to walk away, and I called after her: "Sarah!" She turned and came back. I told her, "Remember this: you are a unique person. There is no one in this world quite like you, and there never will be. You are special!"

She smiled back at me and said, "Thank you, I'LL LOCK THAT IN MY HEART!"

Wow! I guess I was right. She was special!

Chapter 9

That Bloomin' Jacaranda

After the summer of 1958, it was evident to me that the drive-in ministry was successful enough that it was deserving of our full-time commitment. We needed a place where we could stay open year-round, someplace like... well, like Florida. My earlier misadventures in the Sunshine State had planted a seed, and at the right time, God brought everything together.

While in a Youth for Christ convention in Warsaw, Indiana, I met a missionary by the name of Bud Boldt, who lived in St. Petersburg. I told him what I wanted to do, and he said, "Come on down. I'll tell you about some people who might help you with some financing to get you started." Barbara and I prayed about it and decided to build a drive-in theater in St. Pete.

Of course, we also thought, "Where are we going to get money to survive?" We had no idea, except to trust God by faith. We had a trucking company pick up our sixty-five-foot-long trailer and haul it all the way down to St. Petersburg. Barbara went down first and was hired by Trinity College in nearby Clearwater, as their choral director. I stayed at Terry's house for the next week or so, tying up some loose ends. While I was there, I asked Terry to think seriously about coming down to Florida to help us.

It was a hard decision for him to make because he had worked with two churches around Devils Lake for many years. However, because of how effective the drive-in ministry had proved to be, he and his wife Olive felt it was the right thing to do. I was so happy that they made this decision, because I knew the two of us working together could accomplish much more. Trying to start a fire with one log is almost impossible, but if you put two logs together, sparks fly, and so they did.

When we arrived in St. Petersburg, we immediately went to see Bud and his wonderful wife Jo. Then, Terry and I both spent most of our time that year talking to Bud's contacts and anyone else who would listen to us about building a Christian drive-in theater. Of course, most people had never heard of such a thing.

Terry and Olive rented a house, and I prepared a permanent structure for our house trailer. By early 1959, we were finally at a point where we needed to find the right piece of property for the drive-in ministry. Our day would start with Terry and I getting in the car and praying that the Lord would give us wisdom as to whom we should see that day and where the best location for the ministry would be. We both felt that if God wanted this to happen, we should look for the best possible spot and trust Him to provide it. We chose to look on Highway 19, the main artery through town, a divided highway with thousands of people coming and going every day.

Money was no object, because we didn't have any. I have always said that there is a fine line between faith and insanity. I don't know about the insanity, but we sure had the faith. We got hold of a real estate agent and said to him, "Show us ten acres of ground on Highway 19 between Clearwater and St. Petersburg."

He found just the spot, and said, "It's only $40,000."

Well, in 1959 the average annual family income in the United States was about $5,600, but we said, "We'll take it." We didn't have even $40 to our name.

The land was overgrown, undeveloped, and full of brush and wildlife. The down payment on that $40,000 price tag was $7,500, and it was due by the middle of April, just as the brilliant blue flowers of the Jacaranda trees that dotted the area would begin to bloom. We had been working tirelessly over the winter, trying to share the vision and build support, but neither Bud's resources nor any of ours seemed to be bearing fruit. We would receive five or ten dollars occasionally, but that was about it. Our faith was being tested.

April rolled around, and the Jacaranda trees started to bloom, with their brilliant blue flowers. When the day for the down payment to be paid came, we had only $2,500. The agent would have been more than happy to let us out of our contract, for he had someone else who wanted the property and was willing to pay more for it. We had just eight hours left to come up with the remaining $5,000, after struggling for months to come up with half of that amount. We prayed about it, and then jumped in the car, and off we went to visit more prospective donors.

When we got home that night, Barbara was standing at the front door. She said, "Where did you get it?" She didn't ask, "*Did* you get it?" She said "*Where* did you get it?" That's FAITH!

Yes, we had raised $3,000, and another $2,000 had come in the mail that day, donations that had been mailed days earlier. So we got just what we needed and not a penny more. Praise the Lord!

To this day, I still have a dislike for that Jacaranda tree that blooms in April. Fortunately, our banker said our next payment would not be due until June of the next year. It would be $6,200.

We were now owners of ten acres of land with palmettos, pine trees, and rattlesnakes, but at least we had another year to raise the next payment. This was a period of complete reliance on God for our every need, and miracles kept on happening.

In the summer of 1959, Barbara announced that she was pregnant. The doctors had said it wouldn't happen, but it did.

Both of our families went back to Michigan to work at the drive-in there and raise support for our families as home missionaries. Times were tough for us, with very little financial support. Some people would shake our hand at church and leave a $10 bill in it. Others would leave food and milk at our doorstep. At other times, I would go out to the beach and collect small sea shells with tiny mollusks in them and bring them home to make soup. We made soup out of everything. There were times when we would make a meal out of just popcorn. We never missed a Sunday meal—even if we had to wait until Wednesday to get it.

Once the Michigan drive-in season ended, we closed down the ministry there and drove back to Florida, to continue working to raise money and begin the difficult work of clearing the property.

That September, the Florida heat beat down on our trailer... until the temperature inside reached 114°. It was almost unbearable. Our little home had no air-conditioning and was painted black to absorb heat (perfect for a Michigan climate, but not for Florida), and Barb was pregnant.

We needed to find a way to help people understand the vision of the Christian drive-in theater and be able to raise some money. We decided to clear off some of the land, put up a little platform, and invite people to the property to tell them about our plans, about the history behind it and the tremendous potential for reaching people for Christ. We could have them sign a register that we would use later to call on people to try to raise some support.

We also needed a bulldozer operator to come out to the property, push over trees, and level some land. It was time for us to take a step of faith. So, with no money in our pockets, I called a company that had a bulldozer and asked them to come out to the property site. The bulldozer operator spent several hours pushing over trees and digging a small retention pond.

While Terry was talking to the operator, I was standing by the road, when four cars suddenly pulled up in front of me. Five men got out of the cars. One of them was the president of the Christian Mutual Life Insurance Company. Terry and I had spoken many times at the Christian Businessmen's Committee, and this man had heard about us there. The president said to me, "I hear you have an interesting project."

I immediately jumped in and explained the whole program to them. When I got through, the man said, "I like it. I think we all do, and anything we like, we would like to support. Don't you think so, fellows?" They all nodded their heads. Within the next few minutes, they all wrote out checks and handed them to me.

With Terry and the bulldozer operator continuing the work behind me, I wanted to look at those checks right then, but I didn't think it would be very polite, so I just stuffed them into my pocket and thanked the men. After they had gone and the dozer work was done, the operator handed me an invoice for $285. I quickly emptied my pocket, pulling out the checks and totaling them. Those businessmen had given me exactly $285. Again, I learned that God will bless those who trust Him by faith.

By the winter of 1960, we had managed to build a little platform in the middle of the ten acres and invited people to come. We now had a list of names of people we could contact to try and raise money for our next payment, but no matter how hard we worked, we never seemed to raise enough to get ahead. We would accumulate $100 or $200 at a time, enough to purchase printing, stationary, or other supplies we needed in that moment, just enough for the day or the week, but never more. Springtime was showing itself, and that awful Jacaranda tree was starting to bloom. We only had two more months to gather the funds for that payment and, again, we had nothing.

In late March, our son David was born, a happy reminder of God's hand in everything we were doing, but any father could understand the change that comes over you when you have a child to care for. Barbara and I could manage through just about anything, but what were we doing in those conditions with a baby to care for? By the first of May, Terry and Olive left for Michigan to prepare the drive-in there for its June 1st opening. Barbara and I were alone with our infant son in that hot trailer, wondering what God had in mind for us.

Did God really want the drive-in to be built? Was He just testing us? What was going on? We decided that if God didn't want the drive-in, neither did we. It was May 31, and the payment was due the next day. I had a few 3x5 file cards with the names of people who might be interested in helping. There were no millionaires among them. They were just regular, hard-working people. The day wasn't over, so I got in my car and drove to the south side of St. Petersburg to see a lady by the name of Mrs. Chadwick.

Mrs. Chadwick lived modestly in the second floor of a duplex. If I had not been able to raise funds from the many wealthy individuals I had met with over the past year, I had little hope that this appointment would yield any more than a promise of prayers and perhaps a few dollars. I gave the same prepared program I had delivered many times before, but inside my faith was waning. When I had finished, she said, "I'd like to help you."

Discouraged and tired, I said, "Thank you, but today we don't need five dollars or ten. The payment on the property is due tomorrow." I set aside my polished presentation and shared from my heart. "I know you don't have it, but we need $6,200."

Mrs. Chadwick said, "Isn't it something that you should come today? Just this morning in the mail I received an inheritance check." She looked down at the floor for a moment, and then looked back at me. "I think the Lord would have me loan the drive-in $6,000 at no interest. Pay it back when you get it."

I said, "Praise the Lord! Could you make it $6,200?"

Once more she looked at the floor and then looked up at me and said, "No, just the $6,000."

Needless to say, I was excited. I asked her if I might use her phone and reverse the charges to call Terry in Michigan. (There were no cell phones in 1960.) I called and told him the news. He said, "You ugly thing, I could kiss you!"

I said, "It's not the $6,200 we need; it's just $6,000. We need another $200." I said this loud enough so that Mrs. Chadwick could hear it, in case she hadn't understood.

Terry said, "That's amazing! I was standing on the platform just before the program opened last night, when I heard a knock on the door behind me. I went to the door, and there standing before me was a man who said, 'You don't know me, but my name is Robert Royalty. I came here to the drive-in years ago with my girlfriend, and I accepted Christ that night. Years later, we were married and had a baby girl. That little girl recently had a very serious heart operation, and out of all the children who have had that particular operation in the United States, only two have lived. Our girl was one of them. Now we have some insurance money, and I want to give it to you.' And he handed me a check for $200."

I'm always amazed at how God works. After all the pressure I put on Mrs. Chadwick for the other $200, she had listened to the Holy Spirit speak to her. The $200 had already come in. God is never too early, but He's also never too late!

CAPTAIN'S LOG: Irish Rogue

Dateline: Spring 2006 - BELFAST, IRELAND

With Barb in Ireland

For our Fiftieth Wedding Anniversary, Barbara and I received a very nice gift—a trip to Ireland. I had never been there before, and because of my heritage, I thought it was a wonderful gift. Barb's sister Kay and her husband Jon went with us, and we traveled all over that country for a couple of weeks.

I would have loved to go to Scotland, too, because that was where my heritage began. Our family name was changed from Little to Lytle, so that people would forget who we really were—a bunch of horse thieves and murderers who had been kicked out of Scotland! The Lytles settled in Ireland and eventually were kicked out of there too, for doing the same things. They ended up in Pennsylvania, Ohio, and Michigan.

The propellers and rudder of the Titanic in 1912 at the launch site, Harland & Wolff Shipyards [7]

The name "Little" was derived from the fact that my ancestors were small in stature, but I am 6' 4". Obviously, somewhere along the line, someone married the Jolly Green Giant.

I was happy to be in Ireland. The land is beautiful, very green, and the temperature was perfect. It was COLD and WET. We visited all of the major Irish tourist attractions and all of the locations related to the *Titanic*. In Belfast, for instance, we took a taxi to the Harland & Wolff Shipbuilding Company, the place where the *Titanic* was built. I wanted to stand on the exact location where it had been launched into the water.

The property was all fenced in, so we drove around the perimeter, trying to find a location where we could view the spot from a distance. Suddenly, I noticed that a large gate was opening, to allow a delivery truck to enter, and I said to the taxi driver, "Follow that truck!" We pulled up right behind the truck and were able to enter the gate.

The truck was from a catering company, and it was delivering food for some actors who were filming a movie at that location. When I heard that, I got out of the cab and asked one of the men, "Are you making a movie about the *Titanic*?"

"No," he said. "This place is so dilapidated that it makes a perfect set for a murder mystery we're filming."

No matter. We were in!

We drove over to the site where the *Titanic* had been launched, and I was able to stand in that exact spot, as I had wanted. I had seen photographs of this place; one in particular showed a man standing by the enormous port-side propeller of the great ship. Just a few years earlier, on my own dive to the *Titanic*, I had seen that very same propeller, now resting at the bottom of the Atlantic. It meant quite a lot to me to be able to be there at the launch site.

I even went into the famous drawing room where Mr. Andrews and several draftsmen were preparing the plans for the *Olympic* as well as the *Titanic*. The room itself was falling apart, but that famous arch that spanned the room was still intact. I stood there for a while, just trying to make that picture in my mind come alive. Fortunately, there were some workmen inside, trying to bring the place back to its original condition.

There were still pieces of cut tile on the floor, the same tile used on the ship. It was a very unusual tile. Most people of that time had never seen anything like it. When the *Titanic* was being built, there were no restrictions as to cost. Money was no object. It had to be the most luxurious ship in the world. When it came time to put the flooring down on the Grand Staircase, they automatically ordered marble. Someone spoke out and said, "You might not want to do that. There is a new kind of flooring that was introduced at the World's Fair in Chicago in 1892. It looks like marble, but it's very light weight. But, it's also very expensive. It costs more than marble and slate combined, and only extremely well-to-do people are putting it in their homes and hotels."

The White Star Line decided that they just had to have this new product, so they cancelled their order for marble and ordered this instead. When it came, it was just beautiful. It was called "LINOLEUM."

This linoleum was not rolled out in big sheets, like we use today. It was all hand cut, which probably accounted for some of the high cost. So now, pieces of linoleum are scattered about the wreckage of the *Titanic* on the floor of the North Atlantic.

Chapter 10

Billy's Blessing

The more we stepped out in faith, the more we saw God's obvious work, and the greater our faith became. As your faith grows, you can more easily recognize God's leading and become more emboldened to ask for what you want, go farther out into the deep water, take on greater and greater challenges. You still have fear, but God is not held back by our fears. Only we are. You still have obstacles, but you have the wisdom to know that God has a different perspective than you and can lead you around, over, and through any obstacle. Terry and Olive and Barb and I had sure been learning that lesson. Sometimes, though, God just wants to bless you, like a father reaching in his pocket after work to give you something he brought home just for you.

With our payment made, Barb and I took little David back to Michigan, and helped run the drive-in, a pattern we would repeat every summer for years to come. In September, we would return to Florida, to continue the slow process of raising money and building... until the money ran out, then raising more money and building. Step by step, it was happening. That September (1960), Terry and I followed up on a contact with a Florida woman who had the capacity to provide considerable support, one of the last such resources in our area we had not yet reached.

Mrs. Cannon was heir to a retail soft goods dynasty. She wintered on St. Petersburg Beach, but she lived in North Carolina most of the year. We couldn't wait until winter to speak with her, so we got in Terry's station wagon and drove all night to North Carolina. On our way, we went through a little town called Montreat.

Terry said, "I believe Billy Graham lives here. It sure would be nice to see his house."

We stopped and asked a lady where he lived. "Are you ministers?" she asked.

Terry answered, "Yes."

The residents of Montreat were accustomed to such questions and did everything they could to protect the Grahams' privacy, but apparently ministers fell into a different category. She pointed to a road that led up a mountain. "Go halfway up there," she said, "and you'll see his house."

We started up the mountain on a one-lane dirt road. After about two minutes, we thought, "What are we doing? We have no business doing this!" First of all, we had slept all night in our clothes, and our car smelled like an old boxing gym. And secondly, we were about to invade Billy Graham's privacy. We looked for a place to turn around, but there was none.

I said to Terry, "When we get to his house, we'll turn around and go back."

When we arrived, I saw Ruth Graham herself, standing outside trimming her hedges, and she saw us too. We stopped and got out of the car and apologized. "We just wanted to see where he lived," I said, and quickly tried to explain that we had a Christian drive-in theater in Michigan and had many times seen her husband's face on our large screen. "We'll just turn around and go back."

"No!" she said. "He just got back from Africa last night and would love to see you." She turned and went into the house.

A few minutes later, Billy Graham appeared. He was sporting a red shirt and a beautiful suntan and looked bigger than life. As he started walking toward us, I got a stupid grin on my face and blurted out, "THERE HE IS!" Then I thought, "Oh, No!" But I couldn't take it back.

When he came up to us, we shook his hand. I said, "My name is Lowell Lytle."

He then looked at Terry, but Terry was in shock. He tried to say his name twice, but each time it came out backwards, so he stopped trying.

We briefly told Billy what we had been doing and what our plans were for the future. He thought it was a great idea, and he encouraged us and ended our meeting by praying for us. We never did see Mrs. Cannon.

By the end of September, we had been able to clear the land and decided to work together with churches in the area to hold an evangelistic crusade. We planned to put up a large tent on the property, knowing that people's lives would be changed, souls would be saved, and the community would become more familiar with our project and our location. We invited Torrey Johnson, who had started the Youth for Christ program in Chicago and was also instrumental in helping Billy Graham get his start, to be our speaker.

Billy was going to have a crusade of his own in Miami around the same time, but that was more than two hundred and fifty miles south of St. Petersburg. The thought came to us that if Billy was a good friend of Torrey Johnson, perhaps we could persuade him to make a television commercial for our crusade. It sounded like a good idea. The only thing we had to do now was to find Billy Graham.

We discovered that the Miami crusade office was in Fort Lauderdale, and the two of us got in the car and drove across the state—about a four-hour drive—to that crusade office. I asked the secretary, "Where could I find Billy Graham?"

She said, "He's not here; he's fishing today."

"Where is he fishing?" we pressed.

"In the ocean," she replied, accustomed to protecting Mr. Graham as much as she could.

"What color is his boat?" I asked. Our boldness was growing with each step of faith.

She replied, "Apparently you really do need to see him. You might be able to catch them before they leave," and she gave us an address to try.

Sure enough, we got to the place just as the group was loading fishing poles and paraphernalia into a boat. We stopped our car and quickly got out right at the moment Billy came out of a house. He immediately looked at us and said, "The Lytle Brothers." I couldn't believe it. He remembered our names!

Billy agreed to do the television commercial, and at the same time, to do a press event. This all took place a few days later in Clearwater at the Fort Harrison Hotel, just about twenty miles from our property, but about a five-hour drive for Billy and Torrey, and it was a great sacrifice of time for both of them.

When Terry and I arrived that day, we were invited to go up to Torrey's room before the shoot. We opened the door and there sat Torrey and Billy, waiting to discuss with us what they should say in the commercial. After we had hammered out the details, Billy and Torrey spent the next thirty minutes reminiscing and telling us stories from long ago. Then Torrey had room service bring us coffee, but they only brought three cups. Billy poured coffee for the three of us, and then he emptied the sugar packets out of the sugar bowl and drank his coffee from that. I never forgot that experience. What humility!

With Billy Graham at the filming of the crusade commercial

Billy did shoot a commercial for us, and in addition to airing the commercial, we developed a six-week ground-level campaign using mysterious bumper sticker themes to build excitement and interest in the event.

It's amazing what can be done when churches and organizations work together without being concerned about who gets the credit.

With Billy at the filming of the crusade commercial

While area churches spread the word and circulated our bumper stickers, one church had an enormous tent they set up for the event. The result was that three to four hundred people attended each night for about two weeks. Normally, an event like that would be incredibly expensive, but we managed to put on an extremely successful crusade for almost nothing. God was reminding us that His economic rules are different than ours. He can take what little we have to offer and multiply it into something valuable right before our eyes, a demonstration we were to see over and over again.

With the crusade behind us, Terry and I knew we had to get back to fundraising. We spent the whole winter of 1961 trying to raise money for our next payment of $4,500. The blooms on the Jacaranda trees had come and gone, and we were down to the wire again.

A doctor had let us use his vacant office space at Madeira Beach, and while we were there, a lady by the name of Doris Henne came and volunteered her services as a secretary. She would come to our office every day, bringing her sack lunch. I remember sitting with Terry, as we looked out over the water, watching dolphins diving in and out of the surf, wondering, "Where could we possibly get $4,500?"

Then Doris, our modest, unassuming volunteer secretary, wrote a letter to another church up in Michigan, of all places, where she and her mother had set up an account to support ministries. "I don't know how much is there," she said, "but whatever it comes to, you can have it!" As it turned out, it was $4,500. I don't know about you, but that doesn't sound like a coincidence to me.

CHAPTER 11

ROLL OUT THE BARREL

Even though the crusade was free and was not intended to be a fundraiser for the drive-in project, it was a great opportunity for us to tell many people about the future of the drive-in, and because of that, support started to come in, funds we desperately needed to buy materials and rent or buy equipment. Still, we knew we would have to find every possible way to economize, using our own ingenuity, and our own backs, muscles, and hands to build anything great. We disagreed and fussed over which corners to cut and which things were too important to cut, and we learned as we went, and worked extremely hard together, building our dream, our ministry.

We heard that a drive-in theater was being torn down in Tampa, so we went over there to see if we could salvage anything from it. The only thing that seemed salvageable was the steel screen that had been dropped in a pile. We were able to purchase all of the steel for $500, less than scrap price. We had it all hauled to our site and neatly placed it in rows on concrete blocks. Some of the steel was twisted and not usable, but with time and a lot of work, we could make something out of it. They never showed us how to work with steel in Bible college, but we thought, "It can't be all that difficult," so Terry learned how to weld, and I learned how to work the cutting torch. I still have scars on my feet to prove it.

As we worked that year, straightening steel piece by piece and preparing to build, we knew we had to have a plan as to how the drive-in should look. We made some sketches and gave them to an engineer who would know how to design it to keep it standing through hurricane-force winds (125 mph or more). We had rebuilt our Michigan drive-in enough times to know the importance of a sturdy design. He took the measurements of our steel and drew a beautiful plan. Terry and I spent most of our time that year cutting and welding pieces that would fit the plan. We worked day after day in that hot sun all by ourselves, but we were quickly approaching a point where we would need someone else with time and experience, someone willing to work without pay. Of course, God knew this and had already made arrangements for some helpers to arrive. A father and son, Jay and Al Robertson, had come to Florida for vacation. They were just the experts we needed and were also far too industrious to sit on a beach all day, so they became willing servants "sent" to the Sunshine State, not to play in the sand on the beach, but to rescue two exhausted brothers who needed their help.

We had the steel cut and welded together, and we were ready to set the steel supports in place! Well... almost. We still needed a foundation on which to place the steel and a way to lift and secure the supports. We had a solid plan, but the two of us, without expertise and more manpower, were stuck.

The plan called for twelve large anchors to be formed underground, several feet deep. Jay and Al heard about the project, observed our situation, and came to us asking if they could help. "What do you do?" I asked.

"We build missile bases in Minnesota," was their reply.

Hmmm... these men just might know a little something about erecting steel support beams. I've learned over the years that when I am faced with a task beyond my abilities, I shouldn't say, "God, I don't know how to do that!" He already has plans, and He also has people in place to meet our needs. I said, "Great! Here are some shovels. Let's go to work."

We all pitched in, rented a backhoe, and before you knew it, we had twelve large holes in the ground, all of them ten feet square and six feet deep. In the bottom of each hole, rebar-reinforced concrete was poured, one foot thick with four vertical rebars standing up in the center of each.

Now, we needed a way to erect those steel supports and hold them in place, so that the concrete could be poured around them. Another snowbird joined us. Ed Borgman, also from Michigan, owned a gravel pit and was very knowledgeable about construction. He showed us how we could move that steel around without a crane, using only leverage. The year before, someone had given us a truck, so essential to our work. Ed said the truck, a block and tackle, and a gin pole were all we would need. What is a gin pole? It is nothing more than three poles, each about sixteen feet long, leaning together in the shape of a tepee, with a block and tackle hanging from the middle, where they joined.

Fashioning wooden forms to hold the concrete we would pour around the base of those beams was going to be costly. Ed also knew how we could save a lot of money by using old 50-gallon drums, or barrels. When the ends were cut off, and they were stacked and welded one on top of the other, they made a perfect form. Then, they could be filled with concrete. We would need twenty-four barrels, two for each of the twelve steel support beams.

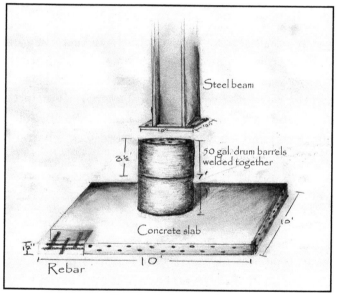

Drawing by Cody Smith

I called three different oil companies and told them we needed used barrels in almost any condition, even rusted or with no ends in them—since we were going to cut the ends off anyway. One of the companies actually delivered barrels right to our property, but they only delivered twenty-three. We spent the next day cutting the ends out of those barrels and welding them together. The last bit of work we did that day was placing the barrels over the rebar we had set vertically on the twelve concrete slabs. These were all plumbed, and we were ready to pour concrete the next day... except for the fact that we needed one more barrel.

John Courts, a local minister interested in the project, was meeting with Terry and me, and the three of us were sitting in our makeshift office that sat next to the highway at around 5:30 in the evening, contemplating where we would go the next morning to pick up a 50-gallon drum barrel, when suddenly we heard: "Bump! Da-bump! Bump! Bump!" We looked out the window and saw a 50-gallon drum barrel rolling toward us. It had fallen off a truck that was on its way to a dump in Oldsmar. The three of us ran outside to pick it up, but the truck driver had already put it on his shoulder and was heading for the truck. I shouted at him, "Where are you going with our barrel?"

He said, "Mis'ta, you don't want 'dis barrel. It ain't got no ends in it!"

I have traveled all around the world, I have been on almost every continent, I have traveled through every state in the United States, and I have been in every province in Canada. I have traveled to China, Singapore, Australia, Norway, Sweden, Denmark, Finland, Holland, Germany, Ireland, Scotland, England, France, Spain, Italy, Greece, Jordan, and Israel and I have NEVER before seen a barrel roll off of a truck in my entire life, and I dare say you haven't either! But God delivered one to us with no ends in it, sixteen hours before we needed it.

My dear brother Terry used to say, "God will honor those who trust Him by faith!" and that particular day He showed us the truth of that saying by reaching over the portals of Heaven with His long arm and tipping a 50-gallon drum with no ends in it into our laps. WE SERVE AN AWESOME GOD! Before the next day was over, the whole frame for the screen was up in the air.

Throughout the year, we continued the construction process, and in November of that year, our daughter Debbie was born, another miracle!

Discussing with Terry the progress on the Florida Drive-in

CHAPTER 12

BLINDERS OFF

With most of the construction behind us, it was time to put the finishing touches on the property and prepare for our opening. Back in the early 1960s, decorative concrete blocks were fashionable, and we thought it would be nice to fill in all the spaces on the backside of the screen with those blocks. The pre-made blocks from the factory were very expensive and too small, so, like everything else on the project, we figured out how to make our own. It took three days to make a mold out of some wood, sandpaper, lots of Bondo wood filler, and elbow grease. We bought a used cement mixer, and wouldn't you know, it worked! Terry and I could make nineteen blocks in a day.

As 1963 dawned and the country's mounting civil unrest rose to take center stage, we continued with the construction project, fundraising and building our vision, step-by-step, block-by-block. By the time we were ready to head back north to the Michigan drive-in for the summer, the violence and protests in Birmingham, Alabama, had reached explosive levels, the news was filled with the atrocities that would become the precursors to U.S. entry into the Vietnam War, and President Kennedy had delivered his historic Civil Rights Address before Congress.

As we finished the summer season and prepared to head back south that fall, to the most segregated part of the country, Martin Luther King inspired a nation with his "I Have a Dream" speech in Washington. While protestors marched in cities throughout the South, we marched forward with our construction work on the property. Our focus was immovable, even as segregation reigned, embedded in the minds and hearts of those around us. I remember that the gas station across the street had a separate restroom for blacks in the back of the building, behind stacks of tires—with no door, no privacy, and no dignity. Our drive-in design had no plans for segregated restrooms, but that was about as far as our involvement in civil rights issues had gotten at the time. Still, the events of that era burned within my heart and would later influence a huge decision still ahead. In those terrible days, however, our resolve to complete the project and use it to reach the community for Christ overshadowed and, in many ways, prevented us from seeing clearly the events unfolding all around us. We had spiritual blinders on.

Throughout 1964, as headlines fluctuated between news from the Vietnam War and the meteoric rise of the Beatles in pop culture, we continued to pound away at those blocks, finish landscaping, install car speakers and make plans for our opening. As our seventh and final year of preparation approached, Barbara and I and our two small children moved out of our trailer and into a real house I had designed and built, just two blocks from the drive-in property. I could walk to work every day. Life seemed good to us, insulated as we were against the war going on around us every day.

There is a lot to be said about those days, a lot that has been said by others. Instead of sharing more political or social commentary, I'd like to take the opportunity to reflect back and make a confession that every Christian from my generation needs to confront and repent of, or, at the very least, spend some time in self-examination about. We were brought up by "the Greatest Generation," with many deep-seated values, but also at least one false and sadly fatal doctrine. Our attitude was that we were "not of this world," as our Bible said, so this world's affairs were not our concern. The politics of the secular world was nothing we needed to worry about.

There was a massive evangelical approach to civil politics that taught people to be completely disconnected from elections and political process, which inevitably lead to a disconnect from the direction of America's social and cultural path. Here is my personal confession: we dropped the ball! We were busy working on our missions and church projects, while the next generation, our children, and our country were left to secular interests that fundamentally transformed the country. We allowed the "Separation of Church and State" doctrine to stand and let the courts drag America off her rightful place as a Shining City on a Hill.

When I was visiting schools in the early 1960s, I saw the Bible being thrown out. I was there when it all started rolling downhill! We all saw it. We witnessed how television programs changed, movies changed, and the music industry changed. While drugs were spilling freely at Woodstock, we sang hymns in our churches and somehow felt that we were above it all.

This is my confession to my children and grandchildren: my generation of Christians was too busy with our plans and projects while their heritage was burning, and we did very little to put out the fire. People were dying, churches were being burned, and kids were going off to war, but Terry and I pressed on with the building of the drive-in, strangely separated from it all. This isn't to say that God wasn't in the drive-in project. Clearly, He was, and He is still using the offspring of that project today. But could we have been a louder voice for human rights and for the shrinking presence of Christian values?

When I heard the news of President Kennedy being shot on November 22, 1963, it shook me to the core and finally broke my singular, isolated focus. I remember clearly where I was standing and what I was doing right then, working on a pump right in front of the entrance to the drive-in, and I had a small AM radio playing in the background. When the news broke, I lost my composure. My knees felt weak, and I slumped over the pump for support. Over the next few minutes, I just cried. Powerful sobs of despair shook my whole body, and I could not go back to work that day.

The dreadful feeling of permanent loss was crushing for everyone. The whole country was in shock. I wasn't mourning just for a president. Rather, I was overwhelmed by the clear understanding that the wholesome innocence of a great nation was forever lost! In truth, it had been slipping away for some time.

Those events burned within my heart and would later influence a huge decision still ahead, but for the moment, life picked up again. We wiped our tears and kept on building, kept on preparing the drive-in, and excused our lack of involvement in the civil injustices of the era with a Bible verse: "Let the dead bury the dead." To a great degree, this book is my attempt to make amends, and to encourage others to take their blinders off, and to take part in preserving the memory of what America was and still can be again.

CAPTAIN'S LOG: TITANIC'S LAST SURVIVOR

Dateline: Spring 2009 - SOUTHAMPTON, ENGLAND

Following our visit to the Harland & Wolff Shipyard, Barb and I and her sister and husband continued our wonderful tour of Ireland. After visiting the city that was once called Queenstown and staying in a castle overnight, we all hopped a plane and flew over to London. Barbara and Kay wanted to see some of the sites there and also to do some shopping.

I had already been to London several times and decided to spend my free time going on a little adventure instead. There were still three people alive who had been on the *Titanic*, and one of them lived in Southampton, about ninety minutes southwest of London. I jumped on a train, and before I knew it, I was at her cottage. My, what an interesting lady she turned out to be!

Meeting with Millvina Dean in Southampton

At 94, Millvina Dean's mind was still extremely sharp, even though she had fallen a few months before and broken her hip, and it was very difficult for her to get around. We talked for the next two and a half hours. Of course, when 4 o'clock came around, we had to have tea and crumpets. Even if the sky is falling, the English must have their tea and crumpets at 4 o'clock every day.

Millvina wanted me to correct an error that had been repeated for many years. She said, "People call me Gladys Elizabeth Millvina Dean. My name is not Elizabeth; it's Elisah. During the war, people called me Gay." Wow, a woman with many names! I promised to try to correct this error for her.

Millvina had been just nine weeks old when the ship sank, the youngest person on the *Titanic*. I asked her if she would tell me something about it. "Of course, I don't remember anything," she said. "I was too young. But my mother told me about the event after I was in middle school. We were in third class toward the back of the ship. My father felt the impact and immediately went up on deck to see what had happened. He saw people running around and knew that something was wrong. He came back and picked up my mother, my brother Bertram, and me and took us up on deck.

"My mother climbed into a lifeboat and was ready for my father to hand me over to her. Worried that I might wiggle out of his grasp and fall to my death, he put me in a bag of some sort. Then he leaned over the railing, handed me to my mother, and stepped back. That was it for him. Mother never saw him again."

"It's interesting," Millvina concluded. "I keep getting invitations to *Titanic* events all around the world, and I keep telling them that I was too young, so I don't remember anything. But if you keep inviting me, I'LL EAT YOUR FOOD!"

Three years later, the Joslyns sent me over to Southampton to interview Millvina again in the nursing facility where she was living. The other two survivors had died, and Millvina was now the last surviving passenger on the *Titanic*. A film crew came down from London and recorded the event.

Millvina was very weak and could no longer walk. She seemed very pleased to see me again, especially when I gave her a little gift, including photos and personal notes the crew in Branson had prepared for her. We chatted for a little while. She told me that her room cost £3,000 a month, equivalent to about US $5,000. She'd had to sell some personal items in order to stay there, items that were found when they were cleaning out her cottage.

One of the items found in a closet was an old bag. "It was very heavy," she said, "as if it were made of canvas. It had a metal clasp at the top and the words 'I.S. New York' written on the side. I remembered seeing it once when I was a little girl. We're going to auction it off."

My final interview with Millvina Dean

I said, "Millvina, that was a mailbag! The RMS *Titanic* was used to deliver mail, so RMS stands for 'Royal Mail Ship.' I bet your father grabbed the first bag he could find, and put you into a mail bag, to lower you off of the ship!"

She said, "I never thought of that."

It was later thought that this particular mail bag could not have been used to lower her to the lifeboat, but it was still a historically significant find. The Joslyns bid unsuccessfully on it in the auction.

Not long afterward, I was traveling with a mobile *Titanic* exhibit out West somewhere and was telling someone the story of how we missed out on the bidding. He replied, "I just heard on the news this week that the man who bought the bag is going to give it back to Millvina." What a nice gesture!

When I got back to St. Pete, I called Millvina to ask if she'd received the bag yet. "No, it's not here yet," she said, "but it's coming." Then she interjected, "I can't talk to you now. I have some visitors here from Pennsylvania. Call me back later." When I got back home a week later, I called the facility and asked to speak to Millvina, only to be told that she had been taken to the hospital with pneumonia. Three days later, on May 31, 2009, Millvina Dean passed away. I still like to think that the bag she had in her possession was the one used to save her life that dreadful night. Why else would her mother have kept it all those years and then passed it down to her?

Once when I was talking to Millvina a few years before she died, I asked her if she had ever received Jesus Christ into her life. She said, "I'm not a religious person. I've tried to live a good life, and I think that's enough."

"You know," I answered her, "the Bible tells us in Isaiah 64:6 that our good works are 'as filthy rags' in God's sight. You seem to be a very nice lady, but our good works are not enough."

After I had shared the Gospel with her that day, she said to me, "You sound like that preacher who comes from the United States to see me from time to time. He's actually going to come here to Southampton and build a church. Can you imagine that?"

Yes, Millvina, I certainly can.

CHAPTER 13

TORNADO!

Throughout the entire building process and our early ministry years, Barb worked as a music teacher at the Bible college, managed through pregnancies under difficult conditions, took care of the children, and somehow kept everything afloat financially—a skill and a responsibility that would become more and more stressful as the years, and the ministry, went on.

Our parents decided, early in the process, that they were willing to leave our home state of Michigan to be near to us, helping us out as they could and, of course, enjoying being near their grandchildren. They moved down just a year or so into the seven years it took us to bring the Florida drive-in to life. Mom and Dad were so happy to be near their children and grandchildren, and we were all settled in Florida, yet we still had a summer drive-in ministry in Devils Lake, Michigan, to run, and other strong family ties and many dear friends still in our home state.

As Easter 1965 approached, Terry and I were entering the last few months of construction, thinking about when we would be ready to open and reflecting back on the difficult road we had travelled to bring the Florida drive-in to life. Then, just a week or so before Palm Sunday, we received a call from Michigan. Our maternal Grandmother Robinson had passed away. Of course, Mom and Dad wanted to fly back for the funeral, but for some reason I didn't feel good about the trip.

"Why?" my mother asked.

"I don't know," I said, "I just think you shouldn't go." The feeling never left me. I took them to the airport, all the while still trying to convince them not to go. In those days, you walked out onto the tarmac and climbed a set of rolling stairs to board the plane. Mom stood in the doorway of the plane, and then turned around and waved to me. I shouted one more time, "I don't think you should go!" She smiled and then disappeared inside, out of sight.

That Saturday, they attended our grandmother's funeral, enjoying the bittersweet opportunity to see family members and catch up with old friends. The next evening, they visited a local church at Devils Lake that was celebrating the Easter season in their brand new building, not far from our drive-in there. The man who put up the money for the new building had said to the church officials, "I'll only give you the money if you build it out of stone. I want it to be around for a long time."

Tornado watches had been posted earlier that afternoon, and a couple of the deacons were joking when they arrived at church, "We're likely to get blown away tonight." Yet no one took the threat seriously. Tornados were fairly common in that part of the country, and unpredictable enough that folks would carry on with their plans, keep their eyes on the western sky, and take shelter only in the last few minutes before a storm approached. Surely, on Palm Sunday evening, nothing would happen to them.

Church members joyously piled into the sanctuary, ready to celebrate and worship together, preparing their hearts and minds for the upcoming Easter week, reflecting on Jesus' triumphal entry into Jerusalem 2000 years before and perhaps on His anticipated return. Mom, for her part, I know, would have been all too sure that Jesus could come back that very night. Throughout our childhood, she had reminded Terry and me every night that our time here on Earth was short. At any moment, the clouds could open up, and Jesus could come riding in triumphantly, as He had so many centuries ago.

Back in Florida, it had been an exhilarating day of worship and celebration for us. We had no clue that earlier in the day one of the largest tornado outbreaks of all time had been churning just north of Tipton, Iowa, and building deadly momentum as it headed due east toward Illinois, Indiana, Michigan, and Ohio. We had planned to spend that evening with Terry, Olive, and their children.

I had no idea just how prophetic my apprehension about my parents' trip would be, or how much danger they were in, even as we were relaxing at home, enjoying Palm Sunday and a much needed day of rest. I had no way of knowing that our Michigan ministry, the drive-in that had started us on our journey, was directly in the path of the oncoming storm. At 7:20 p.m., as our parents stood in a brand new church with dozens of other parishioners, singing Easter hymns, a massive tornado plowed our beloved Devils Lake drive-in into a pile of rubble, before turning its eye further eastward. A second funnel had also formed, just as powerful, and was winding its way directly toward the church where our parents were worshipping.

The pastor was leading singing when suddenly the back door flew open. Two of the deacons managed to pull them shut again, but the tornado was right on top of them. The walls began to move in and out, as people ducked under pews and covered their loved ones as best they could. In just moments, the whole church exploded. Huge stones flew in all directions, injuring dozens and killing twelve worshipers. One of the rafters in the church roof was thrown over a quarter mile away and landed in Devils Lake, as if someone had thrown a big javelin.

Lasting eleven hours, the outbreak formed more than forty tornados, cutting a swath of destruction two hundred miles wide and over four hundred and fifty miles long. With new early-alert systems not fully functioning, most towns were hit without warning. By the time the storm lost its power over Pickaway County, Ohio, more than fifteen hundred people had been injured. Two hundred and seventy-one would die from those injuries.

It was ironic that Terry, Olive, Barbara, and I had decided to get together at our home for a time of fellowship and reflection on the ministry God had given us and to thank the Lord for the success of the work.

What had started as an eight-foot platform in the middle of a cornfield in Devils Lake, Michigan, was now two very successful Christian drive-in ministries, twelve hundred miles from each other. What would be next? Where would these ministries go? What would they turn into? Were they still accomplishing the mission they were built for, to reach the lost for Christ?

At exactly 8:00 p.m., just as we were contemplating our future and marveling at how God was blessing our work, our lives were about to take a dramatic turn. As we enjoyed the last few minutes of the evening, I received a phone call from Michigan: "Both of your parents are in the hospital, and you need to come immediately!"

Terry and I rushed back to Michigan, to our parents' bedsides in the hospital. Both were severely injured, though Mom seemed worse off than Dad. Over the next few days, we spent our time going back and forth between the hospital and the site of the drive-in. Virtually everything in the town of Devils Lake had been shattered into millions of pieces that day. I had never seen devastation like it before or since. Three churches were totally destroyed, including the church our parents had been in, and also our beloved drive-in, the ministry Terry and I had built and labored over for so many years.

About the only building left standing in Devils Lake was a beer garden called "The Timbers." A few days later, Terry was doing some shopping at what was left of the local grocery store, when a local regular at the beer garden came in and shouted to him in a loud, sarcastic voice. "Hey Rev," he said, "What does it mean? Three churches destroyed, but The Timbers is still standing!"

With Terry, surveying the damage at the Devils Lake Drive-in

Terry responded by saying, "It means that in a few years there will be three brand-new beautiful churches and one dumpy old tavern!" He was right. I've always been proud of my brother.

Over the next few days, the doctors did their best, but in the end, Mom would not be able to fully recover from her severe injuries and would need long-term professional care. She was transferred to a nursing facility, where she stayed for many years until she passed away.

During those critical days immediately following the tornado, as Mom's health was declining, Dad was improving. We were actually preparing for his release from the hospital when his condition suddenly took a dramatic turn for the worse. Just three days after the storm had hit, he died from the injuries he had received that day.

It was difficult for me to comprehend why God would take my father like that, but standing next to his casket at the funeral, I had an inner peace, knowing that God knew. He knew my despair, and He knew the why of it all. Of course, that did not take away the human pain. My sorrow was so deep that my heart actually physically hurt, as if I were being crushed. From joy to sadness... that's the roller coaster of life. There are many things we don't understand, but God knows!

We had lost so much in just a moment of time. What could we do to make sense of it all? What would God have us do now? These were questions that would push me toward change in the very near future, but even in that moment we knew we needed to roll up our sleeves and rebuild. This time, we decided to give the Michigan drive-in a more modern look, like its Florida cousin.

The new Devils Lake Drive-in completed

By December of 1965, we finally finished building the Florida drive-in and were open for business, presenting Billy Graham's film, *The Restless Ones*, for our first showing. The end result was that one of the most modern drive-in theaters in the United States was brought into being, and it happened through two brothers with a passion and vision for the ministry and the help of countless others obedient to God's call to support us in every way a ministry can be supported. To God be the glory! Just a couple of months later, Laura was born, our third tiny miracle.

The Florida Drive-in ready to open

The Florida Drive-in, facing the screen

CHAPTER 14

WAY OUT

Devastating loss has a way of bringing you into focus again, reminding you of what's really important in life. We had just been reflecting on our ministry: was it accomplishing its mission of reaching the lost for Christ? I now asked myself, "Is this ministry where I belong?" and I began to explore new avenues for outreach. I had been serving as President and Co-Director of Evangelism for the drive-in ministry, but now I began using my spare time to help other ministries, and as I did this, my vision and my passion expanded. As usual, God knew the end from the beginning. He was leading me right where He wanted me.

I resumed working with Youth for Christ, as well as helping a film producer by the name of Shorty Yeaworth promote his new film *Way Out,* which depicted the power of the Gospel of Christ in the face of the mounting epidemic of drug abuse in America. The film debuted October 25, 1967, and almost every actor in the film was a recovering drug addict.

Shorty was perhaps more famously known for directing *The Blob,* starring Steve McQueen, but his heart was in Christian media ministry, particularly in promoting the power of Christ over drug addiction. Keith Richards from The Rolling Stones once stayed at his home to get help for his own heroin addiction. Working with Shorty on that film was transforming. It was the creeping corruption of morality in an entire generation of youth that now caught my attention and my heart.

Clearly, young Americans were being sold a false Gospel of rebellion and dangerous, self-indulgent behaviors by those who had "won the right to be heard," the folk and rock musicians who had become the gurus of the "Me Generation." In the mid to late 1960s, the United States was in the middle of the Vietnam War, and our own tremendous internal uprising against racial discrimination. We had seen our president assassinated, then Robert Kennedy and Martin Luther King, and hope was rising and falling with the wind. Our youth, assaulted by violent and frightening reality every day, were hungry for the escape that pop culture provided, and they righteously questioned authority and the status quo. They were a fertile field for the powerful influence of the rising culture of "sex, drugs, and rock n' roll."

Movie poster for Way Out

As I became restless for a new direction, looking for anything that would earn me the "right to be heard" among this vulnerable generation, it became apparent to me that a difference of opinion had developed between Terry and me concerning how the drive-in ministry was to be run. We'd already had one major disagreement before our first press conference about what we were going to call the ministry. Terry wanted to call it a "Christian drive-in theater," saying "I don't want to show any films made in Hollywood."

I said, "I think we ought to call it a 'family theater.' We could show some good clean films, like Disney films, and then a Gospel film."

Terry said, "No." I said, "Yes."

He said, "No." I said, "Yes."

He said, "No." We each held strong opinions and convictions as to how the ministry should be run.

I remembered that when we were kids, Dad and one of our uncles had gotten into some sort of argument that made it impossible for us to play with our cousins for a time. I said to Terry, "I don't want that to happen between us, so tomorrow night at the board meeting, I will resign as president and let you run things the way you feel best."

I offered to help him in any way I could, while, at the same time, pursuing a new ministry, performing at high schools in what would become the foundation of what we called "Young American Showcase."

Terry said, "That's very noble of you. Thank you."

The next night, I made a little speech to our board of advisors, and when I was through, Terry spoke up and said, "I've been thinking about it overnight, and I think you need to be here one hundred percent of the time or not at all."

I WAS SHOCKED! It felt like somebody had hit me with a ton of bricks. How could he say something like that with no warning? Barbara and I had spent many years trying to help make this ministry happen.

I loved the drive-in, and it was difficult for me to even think about not being involved at all. But the way things were stacking up, I could tell that it would be almost impossible to work under these conditions. So, for the sake of the ministry, I stepped aside, resigning my position, all the while wondering what God had in mind for Barbara and me.

What I thought might happen happened! Terry and I didn't speak to each other for the next four years. Our children did not play with their cousins that entire time. How sad! Was this my own "way out?" I had been looking for something new, an innovative way to reach our youth. Had God orchestrated this separation? Surely it was He who stirred up my soul and fired up my passion for youth, when I was working with Shorty Yeaworth. Was this God's timing or mine?

Barbara and I were devastated. Terry was not only my big brother; he had become my best friend. Now I was confused, angry, and hurt. The pain in our hearts over our broken relationship with him and his family was excruciating. Suddenly, everything we had gone through to build up that ministry seemed to be all for nothing. Barb had gone without a new dress for eight years, and I had skipped going to the dentist for that same period of time, costing me considerable pain and other health issues. We had invested everything in the drive-in, and now it felt as if all of that sacrifice had been wasted.

This was a very painful reminder that God is not impressed by our good works or our sacrifice. All of those years of toil, working on the drive-in project, had been for us, to teach us patience, obedience, courage, grace, peace, humility, self-control and, above all, to increase our faith. Our sacrifice was not for any future rewards we might enjoy here on earth or even in Heaven. It was for God to use as He saw fit.

Our family in 1966

Very quickly, our financial support dried up, and I had to find work selling palm trees and other landscaping items to help support our family. Barb taught piano from time to time, as she could, to help. At the same time, I began building a new ministry concept through Youth for Christ, but with minimal success at "earning the right" to be heard.

Then, just six months after I had left the drive-in ministry, Terry put up on the theater marquee: "DISNEY FILMS," just as I had hoped we would. Go figure! In defense of my brother, I don't believe he was trying to get rid of me or to control me. I believe he wanted me to be there full time because we had done so many great things together.

Looking back, it is easy to see that God had allowed that breach to come between us so that I could fully pursue my new calling. At the time, however, it was crushing. It wasn't until a few years later that I saw His plan. I could never have orchestrated those events on my own. God is not up in Heaven chewing on antacids, overseeing the little details, trying to keep everything from falling apart. He did not forget about me during that time. No! He knows the end from the beginning. I am His child, and He wants what's best for me. That experience was the turning point in my life; through it, I came to understand what faith rest is all about. Over the course of those dark and difficult months, I had to learn to rest in my faith and rely on God to take care of me and my family.

Although we were not living in an abundance of material possessions, we were experiencing a new kind of spiritual abundance that met all of our needs. The most important part of a puzzle is not the piece in the corner or the piece in the center, or any other piece. It's the box with the picture on top. Only God sees the entire picture, but we can have glimpses of it through the Bible. All He wants me to do is let Him move the pieces around to His liking and just rest in the faith that He knows the full picture. This Christian life is a wonderful roller coaster ride, and I was going down with both arms in the air.

If I were to point out one central theme in the saga of our lifelong calling to evangelism, it would be that we never stopped looking for the next opportunity, the next level of outreach. If there was a better way to reach people for Christ and God gave us the vision to see it, we never chose stagnation. We never said, "What we're doing is good enough." Though we had taken different paths, Terry and I had always attempted to cast the best nets that we could fashion and to throw them where the fish were, a lesson learned early in life from fishing with our father at Little Wolf Lake in Michigan.

Several years ago, I received a phone call from someone whose life had been changed through the drive-in ministry. I came home that night to find this message on my phone answering machine:

"This is Minister James Beezelle, and I'm a member of Shiloh Baptist Church. ... I was telling someone the story of how I got saved and decided to find you and call. I actually got saved about twenty years ago at the drive-in where you were showing those Christian movies, and a couple of my friends got saved as well.

My call is just to encourage you all in the Lord and let you know that the work has been fruitful and a gift that keeps on giving. I just thank God for all of you guys and just wanted to touch base and give you a word of encouragement.

God bless you, and thank you again for being led by the Lord to show those movies, because they had a profound effect on my life."

I thank God for Terry's vision and faithfulness, for my opportunity to work together with him all those years, and for all the lives that were changed as a result. I also thank Him for the decisions that led our paths to separate, for as you will read, He brought two brothers safely through to the other side, all in His perfect timing.

CAPTAIN'S LOG: TITANIC'S LAST HERO

Dateline: Summer 1998 - ST. PETERSBURG, FLORIDA

Barbara gave me a book when I first took the job in Orlando's *Titanic* museum. The title of it was *The Titanic's Last Hero*, and it was written by Moody Adams in 1997. There were a lot of heroes that night. Think of it. They include a Catholic priest who gave the last rights to the very end; the musicians who played comforting music until the last possible moment, considerate of the frightened passengers who were facing imminent death; the men who stood back to let the women and children board the lifeboats first; and the engineers who stayed at their posts to keep the lights on until the *Titanic* slipped beneath the water. These were all heroes, but this one was special. *Titanic's* last hero was a man named Rev. John Harper.

John Harper was a Baptist minister from Scotland, and he was on his way to Chicago to preach at Moody Church. He had thought to take the *Lusitania* but changed his mind and decided to take the *Titanic* instead. One of his parishioners heard about his decision and prayed about it. He later told Rev. Harper that he had an ominous feeling about that ship. He was sure something bad was going to happen to it. "If you'll take the *Lusitania*, I'll even pay for your ticket," he pleaded.

Rev. Harper thought about this and then said, "No, the apostle Paul wouldn't run away from danger. If anything bad happens, I'm ready!"

When the *Titanic* started to sink, John Harper ran about the deck shouting, "WOMEN AND CHILDREN AND UNSAVED PEOPLE, GET INTO THE LIFEBOATS!" You know, it's hard to keep Baptists quiet! With his daughter and sister-in-law standing next to him, he took off his life vest and gave it to a man who was not yet a believer in Jesus Christ, wanting to give him more time to get ready for eternity. The daughter and sister-in-law, both survivors, later testified that he had said to the man, "Take this! I don't need it! I'm not going down; I'M GOING UP!" For more than fifteen hundred people, eternity was about to happen that very night! John Harper then wrapped a blanket around his daughter and passed her along to a crewman to be put on a lifeboat, along with the sister-in-law.

Hero of the Titanic, Rev. John Harper[8]

As the *Titanic* tipped up and took its final plunge, John Harper hit the water, now with no life vest to protect him. The temperature of the water was an icy 28°F, well below the freezing mark. With saltwater, it takes a lower temperature to freeze, but a person could last only ten to forty minutes in such conditions, depending on their will to live and how much body weight they had. All the cries and screams ended after forty minutes. One survivor from Detroit, Michigan, later said, "Every time I went to see the Detroit Tigers play, someone would hit a home run, and the crowd would yell and scream. It was the same sound. I've hated that sound ever since the *Titanic*."

Rev. Harper was treading water in that bitter cold, as hundreds of people screamed all around him. A man drifted by on a piece of wood, and Rev. Harper shouted to him, "ARE YOU SAVED?" The man said, "No!"

Rev. Harper shouted, "BELIEVE ON THE LORD JESUS CHRIST, AND THOU SHALT BE SAVED!"

The man drifted off into the dark, and then a few minutes later the current drew him back. Rev. Harper shouted one more time, "ARE YOU SAVED YET?"

The man answered, "I CAN'T HONESTLY SAY THAT I AM!"

Rev. Harper shouted one more time, "BELIEVE ON THE LORD JESUS CHRIST, AND THOU SHALT BE SAVED!" With that, John Harper slipped beneath the water and passed into the arms of His Maker. There were only twelve people pulled from the water that night... only six of them lived. That man was one of them.

The story was told a few weeks later, in Hamilton, Ontario, Canada, by that same man:

"I listened to Rev. Harper's last message and became a believer in Jesus Christ, with two miles of water beneath me."

Several years ago, I was talking by phone with a good friend of mine, Jack Conners, who was living in St. Louis, Missouri. He was 86 at the time. I told him this story, and he got very excited. "I KNOW THE MAN!" he said. I was incredulous. Up to that point, I had not been able to discover the man's name. "You KNOW the man?" I asked excitedly. "YES!" he exclaimed. "I was playing the marimba for Xavier Cougat's orchestra in New York City when I was 28. I attended Calvary Baptist Church one Wednesday night for a prayer meeting. When they had a testimony time, a man in the back of the auditorium stood up and said, 'I AM JOHN HARPER'S LAST CONVERT!' The pastor, Dr. William Ward Ayer, called him to the platform to share the story."

I was flabbergasted! "Do you remember his NAME? I need to know his NAME!"

Conners paused a moment. "No, I'm sorry," he replied. "I can't remember his name."

To this day, we still don't know the name of John Harper's last convert. I've been telling this story now for more than fifteen years at all the *Titanic* exhibits around the world and have broadcast it live on radio and television stations all across the United States, and all this time no one for whom I have worked has ever told me not to do it. Perhaps it's because it's a true story.

When you read Moody Adams' book, you'll see that Harper had asked the Lord to give him souls to reach. God knew Harper was serious about that. He also knew that the *Titanic* would sink and that many movies, books, and articles would be produced about it, each one building interest in the story. God knew that the technology needed to reach more people with Harper's message of salvation would be increased dramatically these many years later.

God knew that a man by the name of Moody Adams would write John Harper's story in a book entitled *The* Titanic's *Last Hero*. And He knew that I would share Harper's story every chance I got. God also knew that I would include this story in this book. I can't begin to tell you how many millions of people have heard it already. Even though Rev. John Harper died a young man at age of 39, he is still preaching today after more than a hundred years.

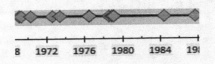

Launching into the Deep

I was starting over. My first aventure out past the safety of the shore had ended, some might say badly, but the experience had built within me the unshakable understanding that I could rely on God completely to provide for me and my family, that He had only been preparing me for my next journey, and I was anxious to get back out into the deep.

Before this period was
over, my life would be in
peril multiple times, by
both man and nature.
I would find myself
in the unlikeliest
of predicaments,
experiencing exhilarating
adventure and deep loss.

CHAPTER 15

NIGHT FIGHT

As I searched for the magic key that would help me "earn the right to be heard" by our youth, I decided to return to my roots in entertainment, this time letting God use my talent as an entertainer to reach young people for Christ. This is what I had prayed on my bedroom floor after the *Horace Heidt Show* so many years before. I began doing magic and ventriloquism in area high schools, inviting the students back to a night show, where I would boldly proclaim the Gospel.

One of the lessons I learned through the drive-in ministry was that human nature causes us to make a snap decision about how much something is worth by whether or not it costs us something. When cars would pull up and see "FREE ADMISSION," they would often turn around and leave, suspicious of anything billed as "free."

When we charged a small fee, they would line up for the chance to get in. I was invited to do a magic show for a high school assembly program in Fort Myers, Florida. I invited the audience to come back the following day for another show across town for a $1 admission, and one hundred and fifty young people showed up. I gave them a

one-hour-and-thirty-minute show, along with a short message. Sixty-five of them received Christ! I knew then that I was fishing where the fish were.

A pastor friend of mine by the name of Dick Erickson said to me, "You need to meet Gary Horton. He's a maverick like you. He's a comedian and a folk singer. If the two of you got together, it would be a killer show."

We met, and my first impression of him was, "This man's tough!" He had muscles that I never even knew existed. We did our first show together in Bartow, Florida, and he was amazing! He had a wonderful voice and played a fine guitar, and oh, was he funny! He nearly had everyone rolling in the aisles with laughter.

That afternoon, we played at a prison, something Gary had done many times before. He would play guitar and sing, I would do some magic tricks, and then he would speak, giving a funny and loving, but also tough and inspiring talk. I felt a little awkward standing in front of those prisoners, with my silk handkerchiefs and feather flowers, but that was part of the show. We played more prisons that year than we did high schools.

Prisoners seemed to like the magic part. I asked Gary one time why they liked it so much. He said, "Are you kidding? You're blowing their minds with your misdirection. They got caught doing what you're doing."

One prisoner came up to me after a show and said, "When I get out of here, we need to get together. With my mind and your fingers, we could make a lot of money!"

The winter of 1969, we performed in prisons and schools in the central part of the state. One day, we were staying in a little town, preparing to do a show at a nearby prison the next day. I went to a phone booth on a street corner to make a call to Barbara, while Gary waited for me in his van. There were about ten cars and fifteen to twenty young men hanging out together in a vacant lot next to me. When I came out of the phone booth and started to walk toward the van, one of the kids shouted an obscenity at me and "flipped me the bird." I ignored him, figuring that these were just a bunch of kids showing off.

I got into the van, and as we drove around the corner past the group, the kid did it again. I couldn't believe it. I thought to myself, "What's happening to our youth today?" And the more I thought about this, the more it infuriated me! By the time we were just about a block away, the little hairs were standing up on the back of my neck, and I said, "Gary, turn around and go back."

"You're crazy," he said, "there's too many of them!" I answered, "I don't care; that's wrong!"

Gary kept on driving, but I insisted again, my Irish indignation rising within me. "No, stop! Let's go back. It's time to teach them a lesson!" Gary stopped and turned the car around, and suddenly I realized that we were about to confront fifteen or twenty kids capable of beating the tar out of us. I was 6' 4" and wearing a large overcoat, but underneath I was still that skinny kid from Jackson, Michigan. I thought to myself, "I need to look bigger," so I grabbed a towel from the back seat and stuffed it under my shoulders, to add some muscle.

Gary said, "Get that towel out of your coat. You look stupid!"

We were almost back at the vacant lot now, and I could see the group still gathered there. I removed the towel and then groped around under the seat, looking for something else to give me an advantage. My fingers closed around a 4-inch diameter pipe. It was about eighteen inches long, and one end of it was wrapped in copper wire. I was still furious, and my indignation and bravado continued to build. As we arrived back at that corner, I jumped out of the van, and Gary was right behind me. I marched right at the middle of the group with that big pipe in my right hand.

I challenged them, saying, "Who's got the big mouth?"

I had no idea what I was going to do or say next. I don't think I had any intention of swinging the pipe, and if I'd had to defend myself, I don't know that I would have been able to do it.

The kid who had sworn at me stepped forward, and in that moment, my heart was pumping out of my chest. Instead of attacking me, he stretched his arms straight out, with hands wide open, and said, "I'm sorry!"

I was left speechless. What do you do after someone says they are sorry? I threw down the pipe, and reached for my pocket.

Imagine those kids, seeing these two older guys march into their midst armed with a lead pipe. Then they see one of them throw the pipe down and go for his side pocket. Surely they must have thought, "One of us is going to get popped tonight, probably the fool who said he was sorry!"

I pulled out a trick pocket knife. (A true magician never leaves home without his props.) "Here," I said, "take a look at this." They had no idea that the knife was rigged, and so they were not anxious to get any closer. Finally, I told them, "This is a magic trick," and in front of their eyes, I made the pocket knife change colors. I went on to entertain them with some coin tricks. Gary told a few jokes and shared his heart with them, ministering and sharing the plan of salvation. It turned out to be a great evening.

I learned something that night, that two little words, "I'm sorry," can alter a situation dramatically. When the boy said that, forgiveness was immediate. All anger and tension disappeared completely. And that is exactly what God wants us to do. He has said, "If we confess our sins, he is faithful and just to forgive us our sins and cleanse us from all unrighteousness" (1 John 1:9). What a great lesson!

A few years later, I reached out to Terry, having already forgiven him in my heart. For his part, he apologized for what he had said and done. It took me right back to that night in 1969 when that young man on the street corner diffused my temper with those two little but powerful words, "I'm sorry." From that moment until Terry's death in 2008, we were like the brothers we used to be.

Even during our separation, we were both right where God wanted us. As I pursued a new direction, Terry continued to run the drive-in ministry and eventually developed a mobile pop-up theater that could be driven to the most remote places of the world, allowing transforming movies to be shown to people never before reached. When the movie *Jesus* was released, these vans were shipped overseas, where they brought the Gospel to remote villages and towns that had never before heard such a powerful message.

Each van also had a small platform that could be erected in just a few minutes for a speaker or singer to use. Sometime in the 1980s, I joined Terry to travel with the van ministry to Ukraine. I had been singing in a Southern Gospel quartet, and the whole group travelled overseas to be part of sharing the Gospel through this unique van ministry. This group would sing off and on for the next five years, going from city to city, ministering to people who had never seen an American before. In some cases, we were singing and speaking to people who had been told for generations that there was no God.

The Ukraine van ministry in action

Terry's vision turned out to be a wonderful ministry that resulted in one hundred and twenty churches being established in Ukraine and other unreached places, and I was proud to be a part of it and to be able to serve the Lord side-by-side with my brother again.

CHAPTER 16

FACING THE KLAN

Playing for prisoners was one thing; they were literally a captive audience, but if we were to win the right to be heard among young people who had a choice about whether or not they wanted to attend our show, we would need to kick things up a notch. What was it we were missing?

A drummer by the name of Buddy Waterman joined our group, and for the next year we played junior and senior high schools. Every night, there would be two to three hundred young people who would make decisions for Christ. Young people were desperate for the one answer that could give them security and peace in an unstable and volatile world, and this was our time to oppose the influence of the pop culture messages of rebellion and experimentation with "sex, drugs, and rock 'n roll," by fighting fire with fire.

We decided to add more members to our group and form a full rock 'n roll band, playing Top 40 music that would appeal to teens and taking our approach of "underground evangelism" directly into the public schools of America. In the 1970s, just as today, you could not pray, read the Bible, or evangelize in any way in a school building when classes were in session.

After school was over for the day, however, we were free to speak out. We would entertain students with their own pop culture at high school assemblies throughout the area during the day, to draw them back for a hard-driving, entertaining night show, and then share the Gospel at the end of the evening. We were determined to counter the "counter culture" by winning the right to be heard among our youth. In this way, the foundation for Young American Showcase (YAS, as we called it) was laid.

Terry Casburn, Lowell Lytle, Joe Brown,

First Free Fare

Gary Horton, Wayne Hackett & Henry

A reproduction of the first Young American Showcase show poster

You can imagine that, having been raised in a deeply conservative family, it was a little difficult for me to go from folk music to rock 'n roll. I personally had a dislike for rock 'n roll, as did many Christians. Almost all of my Christian friends now thought I had gone off the deep end, and I faced a lot of resistance from church leaders.

In the 1960s, the Christian culture generally believed that rock 'n roll in itself—the beat, tempo, and the VOLUME—would incite young people to rebel and to commit all sorts of sinful acts. Church leaders would insist, "It's that devil beat!" Personally, I never quite understood how they could believe that a beat could make someone do something evil. All music has a beat. The old hymn "Holy, Holy, Holy, Lord God Almighty" can be sung to a disco beat. In my heart, I knew that it's what you say in the music that makes the difference, not the music itself.

Gary Horton was very good with a guitar, but he could never really play rock 'n roll, so our first band ended up playing soul music. Gary had been critical to the early success of Young American Showcase. Anyone who could stick with me through the money-raising process, would use his own money to pay principals so that we could put on an assembly program in their school, and who would sleep on the kitchen floor in someone's home beside their noisy, rattling refrigerator, had to be a trooper. Gary was all of that and more. He performed well in the first band.

After that first year, however, he made a decision to join the Army and became a US Army Ranger, one of an elite group of heroes. When he left the service, he immediately went back to ministering in prisons and high school assemblies across the United States, and as of this printing, is still doing it.

Along with Gary on guitar, in that first band, we had Wayne Hackett on drums, Joe Brown on keyboard, and Terry Casburn playing the bass. My part was to play the tambourine, sing along, and perform magic and ventriloquism with my dummy, "Henry."

We travelled north during the summer, to practice on the grounds of Michigan's Ionia Free Fair in their floral building. During that first summer practice camp and fall tour, we all stayed on the farm of Barb's family. The name Ionia Free Fair inspired us to name our group "Free Fare," and the name was indeed inspired. The spelling of Fair changed to Fare because our message of salvation was free.

More than eight hundred young people attended our first evening show, and the next day there were more than thirteen hundred. The show was a success!

We traveled around Michigan for a few months, and then we moved back to Florida before winter set in. We were doing quite well... until we came to an old fishing village called Port St. Joe. Today, I'm sure, Port St. Joe must be a wonderful city that embraces every culture, but back then, in the late 1960s, it was a town much like every other small southern town—thick with racism and conflict.

When we arrived at the high school in Port St. Joe, the principal took us into his office, pulled out a drawer in his desk, and showed us some knives and chains he had there. He said, "This is what some of the kids brought to school today, and the blacks are boycotting the school because there was no black cheerleader chosen to be on the cheerleading team last week." That night's audience, due to the boycott, would be all white.

Keep in mind that our first band, purely because of lack of ability to play rock 'n roll, was playing the soul music of Aretha Franklin, James Brown, Little Richard, and all of the other greatest R&B artists of the day. We were all white, but we played what was thought of as "black" music. Wayne Hackett, our drummer, listened to soul music day and night, preferring its driving rhythms to the more predictable beat of traditional rock 'n roll. Gary Horton had been brought up on the south side of Indianapolis, immersed in the African-American culture. He carried himself with the recognizable pride and confidence he saw in his black peers. How would a white audience in a deeply divided city react to us?

We had picked up a new lead singer, Danny Skidmore, while we were in Fort Lauderdale and added him to our group. Also white, he had been the choir director in a primarily black church, leading worship with songs that were literally the backbone of soul music. He was accustomed to singing in a style well loved by his black brothers and sisters at church.

Now, try to get the picture: we were about to do an assembly program in front of young white people, most of whom had been brought up with racism and were all struggling with the racial conflict that had been building in their community. The curtain opened, and we began playing "Knock on Wood" by James Brown. Our lead singer tucked both of his thumbs under his belt, glided across the stage on one foot, doing a James Brown impression, and shouting, "EEEE YAHOOOOU! AIN'T IT FUNKY NOW?" The kids looked at us as if we had turnips coming out of our ears. We didn't care and just kept right on playing.

The time came in the show for Gary to do a ten-minute comedy routine. Now, there's something you need to know about Gary: he had a short fuse. All the wires were hooked up, but the insulation had been burned off. I never knew if he was going to shake a principal's hand or punch him in the mouth. One thing was certain to him: right was right and wrong was wrong, and these kids were wrong.

He started his "comedy" routine by saying, "I see you ran all the blacks out of school today."

The kids applauded and cheered.

Gary said, "I didn't mean that as a compliment! What's the matter with you people? This is the twentieth century. You should be ashamed of yourselves."

He continued to rip on them for ten minutes, and then we played some more soul music. After the assembly, a group of about fifteen kids wanted to fight us, so we quickly left the building.

The next evening, when we came back to do the night show, there were five police cars at the school to greet us. One officer told us, "Whatever you do, get into the school quickly and stay away from windows because the Ku Klux Klan is going to march on you tonight." We couldn't believe it, but sure enough they did.

I believe all eight hundred kids came back to the night show, many hoping to see some blood. While we were performing, the Klan marched outside of the school. After the show, while we were signing autographs, some of them came inside and marched down the aisles carrying plaques that read, "FREE FARE, N_____ LOVERS" and "FREE FARE, GO HOME ." They had burned a cross in the black section of town during the show. The police gave us an escort out of town that night. They went in front of us and also behind us, with their red lights flashing. We never went back to that town.

As we began to improve the program and understand how powerfully God was using this little group, we also quickly realized there was an entire country full of students to reach. We were going to need more bands and a way to prepare them for the road. Somehow, we had to find a way to expand, and to pay for equipment and transportation, and also a way to support the guys while they were on the road. We would need someone to book shows and make all of the arrangements and, of course, someone to manage the money.

Our dining room table served as the office throughout those years, and Barb served as the faithful manager. She was also teaching and taking care of the kids, while I was performing. She often stayed up after the children had been put to bed, working on the books until well past midnight. God had surely known what I needed when He brought Barb into my life!

As we continued to take our band around, we spread the word that we were auditioning for new members. Soon we had hundreds of audition tapes to listen to, for about twenty positions. Very quickly, we were up to four bands, each performing roughly the same show in different states at the same time.

We established some basic rules of behavior: if you broke a rule, you had a consequence, and if you didn't straighten up, your days as a rock star were over. These bands were on a mission, and each member's every move would be watched by the students and community. Any moral failure on their part had the potential of ruining our "right to be heard," and we had fought hard to earn it.

Next, managers were hired, spiritually strong men capable of keeping a bunch of headstrong, star-struck musicians united and focused while they were on the road. It was all quite an undertaking.

CAPTAIN'S LOG: SHANGHAIED!

Dateline: August 2004 - SHANGHAI, CHINA

In 2004, RMS *Titanic* opened a traveling exhibit for the first time in Shanghai, China, and I was asked to go there for the opening. I flew from Tampa to Tokyo via Detroit and then from Tokyo on to Shanghai—a trip of nearly twenty-four hours. As I boarded in Detroit, I carried my uniform in a clear plastic hanging bag, which the stewardess hung for me in first class, while I took my usual seat in the coach section. A few minutes later, she came back to ask me about the uniform and who I was. "Your uniform is better than our own captains' uniforms!" she laughed.

I told her that I was E.J. Smith, captain of the *Titanic*. Then, with a twinkle in my eye, I explained that I was an actor going to the opening of the *Titanic* exhibit in Shanghai, to portray the captain. She left for a few minutes and then came back to tell me, "The captain of the *Titanic* can't be sitting back here in

As Captain Smith, posing with workers at the Chinese Titanic exhibit

the coach section. Follow me." For a few hours of that difficult trip, I was able to stow my long legs and 6' 4" frame in a more comfortable FIRST-CLASS seat. It was exceptional that the Chinese government had allowed the movie, *Titanic,* to be shown in that country.

Now, I would be at the *Titanic* exhibit in China with an official interpreter at my side, and I would be telling all the stories I tell at other museums around the world, including the story of *The* Titanic's *Last Hero.* Over a two-week period, I would share the Gospel of Jesus Christ in a place where talking about the Lord could get a person thrown into prison. Over and over again, throughout each day, I would talk about Jesus, tell the John Harper story, and finish with that biblical phrase, "Believe on the Lord Jesus Christ and thou shalt be saved!" All the while, my official Chinese interpreter was repeating in Mandarin everything I said for the crowds. There were no restrictions, and no one asked me to stop.

There are many interesting stories I've told to museum visitors about second officer Charles Herbert Lightoller, the highest ranking crew member to survive the shipwreck. After the ship went down, a board of inquiry was established in New York to investigate the reasons for the tragedy. Officer Lightoller was asked, "When did you leave the ship?"

"I never left the ship!" he insisted.

"Then did the ship leave you?"

"Yes sir!" he answered, "A huge wave washed me overboard, and I was immediately sucked down to a grid that went to Boiler Room Six. I could not breathe, I could not move, and it felt like a thousand knives stabbing me. The first thought that went through my mind was Psalm 91:11: 'He will give his angels charge over thee and keep thee in all thy ways.' I no more than thought that, when the boiler exploded and propelled me like a rocket to the surface, right next to a lifeboat!"

The survivor accounts from the *Titanic* disaster, like all of life, were filled with near hits and misses. One small error could, and did, change the course of history.

Captain Smith was the wealthy man's captain, meaning that he schmoozed well with the rich. Many first-class passengers would not even sail across the ocean without Smith at the helm. He had been planning to retire on the *Olympic*, the *Titanic's* sister ship, but I'm sure his wealthy friends must have applied lots of pressure on the White Star Line to get E.J. to come out of retirement long enough to make the maiden voyage of the *Titanic*. At the last minute, he said, "I'll do it... if you'll let Officer Wiles be my chief officer." (Wiles had been the chief officer on the *Olympic*.)

The White Star Line agreed, but that meant one officer after another would be bumped down a level. Wiles bumped Murdoch to 1st officer, Murdoch bumped Lightoller to 2nd, and so forth, until the 4th officer said, "Let's stop this domino effect. I would like to be on the *Titanic* for my resume, but I'll take an assignment on the Oceanic." He walked off of the ship just an hour before it sailed from Southampton, purportedly with the key to his *Titanic* locker still in his pocket. In that locker were the binoculars for the crow's nest.

Many people ask me what happened to the *Olympic*. She served well for many years. In fact, she became known as "Old Reliable" and was used as a troopship during World War I, actually running over and sinking a German submarine. It is very possible that my own father was on the *Olympic* as a World War I soldier. By the time he got halfway across the ocean, the war had ended, so his ship turned around and came back to the U.S. Had the war not ended when it did, I may never have been born.

In 1934, the *Olympic* hit a lightship off of New York Harbor, killing seven people. Because of its relationship to the *Titanic*, the ship naturally got a lot of bad press. So, in 1935, it was decommissioned and taken apart. Pieces of it can be found in hotels, restaurants, and museums all over the world.

One of the *Titanic's* third-class passengers, Jeremiah Burke from Queenstown, Ireland, was given a bottle of holy water by his mother before he left on the voyage. Perhaps she thought it would protect him. When the ship started to sink, it was evident to Jeremiah that he would not be able to get into a lifeboat, so he emptied the bottle of water and then wrote a little note, rolled it up, and put it into the now empty bottle. The note read, "From Titanic: Good-bye, all." He put the cork back in the bottle and threw it into the water.

Jeremiah did not survive, but exactly a year later, that bottle rolled up on the beach in Queenstown. Someone found it and gave it to the local newspaper. A day later, his mother read an article that had been written about it. She went down to the office and confirmed that it was the bottle she had given her son, and that it was his signature. That bottle and note were treasured by the Burke family until 2011, when they donated it to The Cobb Heritage Center, a local museum.

As the *Titanic* was sinking, the officers had a hard time convincing people to get into the lifeboats. It was so cold outside and so dark, and the ship was so warm and "unsinkable." One of the crewmen was trying to get the third-class people to come up on deck. He banged on one of the doors, and a lady opened it. "Lady, get aboard the lifeboats; the ship is sinking!" he pleaded.

"No," she declared, "I'm going to stay in here where it's safe." Then she shut the door and locked it. WOW!

When I heard this story, I couldn't help but see a parallel to our own path to salvation. God says, "There is a way that seems right unto man but the ends thereof are the ways of death" (Proverbs 16:25).

CHAPTER 17

ONLY LANCE!

Organizing and preparing more and more groups to tour the country every fall required an incredible amount of effort. While work was going on feverishly behind the scenes to book shows, prepare transportation, and close every possible administrative and financial gap, we held a rehearsal camp at a college campus in Sarasota, Florida, to prepare band members for the road. We could teach routines and music, and we could set ground rules, but in just a couple of weeks, it was much harder to teach a group of guys who had never met before how to entertain, capture the audience, work as a unit, and win the right to deliver the Gospel. Throughout all of this, the original band continued to perform.

We were staying at a motel in St. Petersburg called "The Office," getting ready for our evening show, when we heard some musicians playing in another room. A rock band called "The Fabulous Entertainers," a professional group that had played in big entertainment venues around the country, was rehearsing for their next show at a nearby nightclub. We talked to them a little while, and after some friendly conversation, they said, "You might want to come and see us perform some time." Well, I wasn't excited about going into a nightclub to see a band. As a young ventriloquist, I had performed in my share of nightclubs, and I didn't want to return to that atmosphere. But if we were going to see them, that's where we had to go.

When we walked into the place, I couldn't believe it. The band was playing the song "I Wanna Take You Higher," and there was so much energy on that stage that the audience couldn't sit still. People in their fifties and sixties were standing on chairs and tables. It was amazing!

Jerry Heard
Atlanta

RODGERS AGENCY
P.O. Box 80339
Atlanta, Georgia 30341
(404) 457-1376

The Fabulous Entertainers

The Fabulous Entertainers promo shot

After the show was over, I went to the dressing room, and they were all sitting on the floor, drenched in sweat. They had given everything they had in that show. I said, "Who's the leader of your band?"

One of the band members pointed to Lance Abair, the keyboard player. By this time, we had about four groups on the road, and I asked Lance if he would be willing to come down to our rehearsal camp for three days and teach our young men how to perform like that. He agreed, and that was the beginning of our understanding as to how rock 'n roll music should be played. What a talent Lance was!

A year later, I heard a knock on my front door, and when I opened it, there stood Lance Abair. "I enjoyed teaching your guys at the rehearsal camp last year," he said, "and now I would like to join your organization." Well, in a ministry like that, we often had young musicians who were new to their faith, not strong enough to be able to live godly lives in the midst of extremely challenging work, and surrounded by temptation and by students who idolized them—literally. We knew that adding someone to the staff who didn't share our faith would be a critical mistake, but I said to Lance, "Come on in, and we'll talk about it."

Over the next few weeks, we spent a lot of time "talking about it." Lance knew he couldn't just "fake it," but he also wasn't ready to believe that he could have a personal relationship with God. He called me several times that summer, and each time he would say, "I really want to do this."

I would always answer, "I'm sorry."

The last time he called, I said, "I'll tell you what I'm going to do. I'll let you come down to rehearsal camp for one month, but I can't put you on full time." He agreed to come.

At these rehearsal camps, we brought in more young men than we actually needed, knowing that some of them wouldn't work out. We told them at the beginning that not all of them would make it, but no one wanted to be sent home. We always took time for spiritual devotions. We would all gather in the auditorium each day for about thirty minutes, and Don Kenyon, our spiritual advisor for the first three years, would speak to us. Lance, as part of the staff, was there, listening to everything that was being said.

After these devotion times, we would dismiss the group, but the rest of the staff would stay to listen to more individual auditions and try to discern if each person trying out was a genuine Christian. One of these hopefuls was a keyboard player from Pennsylvania. He had long blonde hair and wore a ring in his ear. He was a very good performer, and we really needed him, but after questioning him from every angle, we could all see that he was not a believer. None of us said anything.

It was now about 12 o'clock, and Barbara had lunch ready for us in the cafeteria. The staff jumped into a truck to drive over there, and

Lance blurted out, "There was something wrong with that last guy, wasn't there?"

We all chuckled and said, "Yes."

It was customary that the staff would eat lunch together at the same table, so we could discuss important things. During the discussion that followed, I said, "We need to get rid of that guy and bring in another keyboard player."

Don Kenyon said, "Let's wait a while. God has him here for a reason. The Bible says, 'Lay hands on no man suddenly.' Let's give it a little time."

The following day, during lunch, I said, "Somebody needs to talk to him."

Now, you need to know that, in addition to being a great musician, Lance had an off-the-wall kind of humor. He popped up and said, "I'LL DO IT!" We almost fell out of our chairs with laughter. Lance would be the last person to talk to this young man because he himself had not yet given his life to Christ.

It was obvious, after a few days, that this keyboard player would not work out. Lance watched us all through this process, slowly learning, and seeing for himself the importance of a spiritual foundation, the reason why members of these groups had to have Jesus as their common ground. He had yet to experience, however, the power of prayer and the divine intervention of God.

Lance was great at working with the performers and felt the responsibility to make each group work. Letting go of a musician he knew would be a fantastic performer was frustrating for him. We were already a week into camp, and we still needed a keyboard player. Finally, Lance started to freak out. With a look of panic on his face, he said to me, "What are we going to do? Where are we going to find another keyboard player?"

"I don't know," I said, "but God knows! Get in the car; we're going to watch a miracle happen."

LANCE: "Where are we going?"

LOWELL : "We're going to Dunkin' Donuts on the south end of

Sarasota. They have a telephone booth outside."

LANCE : "Who are you going to call?"

LOWELL : "I don't have the slightest idea, but we'll just pray about it."

I prayed a short prayer, asking God to give me wisdom to find the right keyboard player. The first thought that came to my mind after that prayer was Allen Metzger, the Youth for Christ Director in Kansas City, Missouri. Don Kenyon had sent me there for a training program way back in 1955, when I was working with him at the Lansing, Michigan Youth for Christ program.

Keep in mind that in 1970, rock 'n roll was considered "the devil's music." I knew it would be hard for him to fully understand and support what we were doing, but I felt that he was the man I was to call anyway. I called from that phone booth and explained what we had been doing over the past several years and how effective it had been. Then I said, "I need a keyboard player. Do you know of someone who might know of someone who knows of a keyboard player?" Within forty-eight hours, we had another Christian keyboard player in our camp, and Lance was convinced that he needed to figure out what this Christianity was all about.

LANCE : "Man, I've got to get this thing nailed down."

LOWELL : "Good! At 10:30 tonight, right after practice, meet me here under the street light, and I'll introduce you to the Lord."

At 10:30 sharp Lance came walking down with his little satchel under his arm, as if he was ready to take care of some official business. And indeed he was.

LANCE : "Okay, what do I have to do?"

I shared God's plan of salvation with Lance that night, and he invited Jesus to come into his heart. Right after his prayer, you could see a change come over him.

LOWELL : "Lance, the angels in Heaven are rejoicing because of what you just did!"

LANCE : "Good, I like to start parties." Only Lance!

When you first become a Christian and fully understand the peace that comes with knowing that you have eternal security, in the next breath you realize your loved ones who don't know the Lord are in grave danger, and you can't wait to share with them, to give them the key to their own salvation. Lance, of course, immediately thought about his wife Linda and went home right away to talk to her. Three days later, he returned, his wife now joining him in his peaceful submission to Christ. Lance joined our staff full time and threw himself into learning about his newfound Savior with everything he had.

Lance in the YAS office, hunting new talent

When the groups left camp, Lance and I got on an airplane, to go and critique them. If I picked up a magazine on the plane to read, Lance would pick up the Bible. When we got to our motel room, I would turn on the television, and Lance would immediately turn it off, pick up the Bible, and say, "Where do I start?"

Everything this young man did was 110%, so why should his faith be any different? Not only did he grow quickly in his understanding of the Gospel, he began sharing his faith immediately, first with his own wife, then with everyone else he met.

Much of what Lance did in the office was finding new talent and then auditioning them on the phone. If he discovered that the musician was not a Christian, he would say, "I'm going to send you some literature. Read it. I don't know much about this, for I'm kind of new at this myself, but when the Holy Spirit does a tap dance on your forehead, just give in!" Only Lance!

So many of us fail to share the Gospel because we're afraid we don't know enough about it to be able to share it or to defend our beliefs, or won't have the right words to say. How refreshing it was to see someone so new in the faith be so bold!

After Young American Showcase, Lance went on to have a great career, as did many of the members of Showcase. Now we are seeing the children and even grandchildren of Showcase members carrying on in their parents' and grandparents' footsteps, either in music, ministry, or in leadership roles in business and the community.

Lance performing with his daughter, Mindi Abair

I left the road as an entertainer completely in 1972, and when I wasn't running the company or working on a new project, I spent my time critiquing the bands. That job was much harder than performing. I knew what had to be done, but I couldn't be on stage to make it happen—which was extremely frustrating. I would sit in the audience with a small tape recorder, taping every mistake a performer would make. Then, at the end of the show, I would run backstage and play it back for them, giving them instructions, all the while trying not to hurt their feelings.

Nobody enjoys being critiqued, but to save the show, it had to be done quickly before the next group of kids came into the auditorium. Many times, at the end of a show, I would reach my hand into my armpit to see if it was wet. If it was, I had a lot of critiquing to do.

Whenever you are in the middle of something God is doing, when you let yourself be His to use as He sees fit, when you take a step of faith, a risk, when you pray every day for His guidance, you can count on two things:

(1) Obstacles will get in your way, either because of your own wrong choices or because of circumstances or powers at work against you, and

(2) Miracles will happen to help you along. You'll know you are in the right place when you can see God working and witness lives being changed—especially your own.

When Young American Showcase had started, its purpose was to fight fire with fire, to bring Christ to a world of lost youth through unconventional means. All of the people involved in this ministry got a chance to experience some amazing things and see countless lives changed. Back at the home office, we would hear stories that were heart-stopping, incredible, or sometimes just plain funny... like the story of angels in Alaska.

CHAPTER 18

ANGELS IN ALASKA

Once in a while, Showcase would bring to camp an entertainer who seemed to have the potential to give you problems on the road. They were talented, but you weren't quite sure if you could trust them. There were several of those over the twenty-year period. One who comes to mind was Stan Arthur.

Hired as a drummer right out of high school, Stan began to show his "potential" during rehearsal camp. A few of us sat him down to talk and showed him some "tough love." I explained our concerns, ending my little speech quite dramatically: "If you mess up, I'll be your worst nightmare!" As I had been talking to him, I didn't realize that I was playing with a plastic spoon. When I said the words "worst nightmare", my fist closed and I snapped that spoon in half, making everybody in the room jump.

One of the managers later said, "If you put him in my band, I quit!" Wouldn't you know it, that was the band where Stan was placed.

Fortunately, this manager didn't quit. He worked with Stan for a year, knocking off the tough edges, only to discover a diamond in the rough. Stan went on to work with Showcase for eleven years and proved to be one of the most dedicated employees I ever had, and a very good friend. He also grew tremendously in his Christian faith over those years, as God used him on the road (as you will see in this next story).

It was Stan's eleventh year in Showcase, not counting a one-year sabbatical during the "84-85" tour. He had been an Associate Director since the fall of 1980, touring with his wife, Carren, from band to band, fixing the shows and reinforcing the show concepts the rookies had been taught during rehearsal camp. By the summer of 1987, he had convinced me to allow him to once again perform full time and to manage a group of a few hand-picked musicians, Showcase veterans who knew the concepts better than most. By mid-August, Stan's Free Fare band was rehearsed and ready, and they immediately left to begin a month-long tour of Alaska. Here is Stan's account of what happened during his very last year with Showcase:

After a few days playing shows in the Juneau area, we had to make a twenty-four-hour trip to Fairbanks. The first leg was a seven-hour ferryboat ride from Juneau to Skagway, then it would be over the road to Fairbanks. If you Google it today, you'll see that it's about a fourteen-hour trip under good conditions. The other thing you'll notice is that you'll be passing through the Canadian Yukon. You'll also notice that there are no towns on the map between the two cities.

We were driving a very large tour van called an "Iveco" that held the band members up front and all of our equipment in the back. There were eight of us and a 7-year old Eskimo dog named Annie making the trip. I decided that I would take the wheel for the first part of the journey overland.

Fuel mileage was poor on the Iveco, and we had hundreds of miles at

View from the Iveco, on the road to Tok, Alaska

a stretch with no gas stations in between. I remembered seeing a small town called Tok on a map we had, about a hundred miles east of the Yukon's western border, still about two hundred miles from Fairbanks. According to my calculations, we would have enough diesel fuel to make it to Tok, but not much further. We would have to find fuel in Tok. That much was certain.

In that part of Alaska, during mid-August, there are about nineteen hours of daylight, from approximately 6 a.m. to 11 p.m., a useful fact to know when driving in unfamiliar territory. We exited the Skagway Ferry and started on our way by 11 a.m., needing to be in Fairbanks for an 8:30 a.m. show at a high school the next morning.

The sky was grey and misty, with an occasional drizzle that put just the right amount of foreboding on our circumstances. The road was a sometimes-treacherous mix of conditions—part paved, part dirt and gravel. I could tell right away that it was going to take longer than we had anticipated.

I drove for eight hours straight before becoming too weary to continue. Along the way, there had been very few signs of civilization. At that point, I recalculated and figured we still had eleven hours to go. We would be cutting it close, but should still make it on time. I turned the wheel over to Ron, who was kind enough to volunteer to drive, and told him in no uncertain terms that we would not have enough fuel to make it all the way to Fairbanks.

We would have to find fuel in Tok. I settled back in one of our super-comfortable captain's chairs and fell (almost immediately) into a deep slumber, the kind of sleep that takes you on a journey far, far away from your reality.

I was floating and flying over beautiful landscapes, lighter than air, without a care in the world, enjoying the company of all my friends, doing things I loved to do back home, and I was enjoying the sweet, sweet rest of one who had endured much duress over the course of the last few weeks. Then a small fly began to buzz in my head with a familiar sound. Bzzz ... bzzz ... bzzz ... and then the "buzz" became a word... then the word became a name ... Stan ... Stan ... STAN! Ron, still driving, was trying to wake me up.

When I finally came to, Ron said, "We're going to run out of fuel!"

"How can that be?" I asked. "How far is it to Tok?"

"We passed that place a couple of hours ago," he said, "and there was nothing there."

"What do you mean, 'there was nothing there'?" I said, incredulously.

"I mean there was a sign that said 'Tok' and nothing else. No gas station ... no store ... no nothing!"

I said, "Oh my goodness, how long have I been asleep?"

"Eight hours," he said, "and we still have about three hours to go. I did see a sign for a town in about fifty miles."

"I take it we're not going to make it that far," I said. "I don't think so," was his answer.

We made it about another twenty miles before the engine stalled. We coasted to a stop around 3 a.m. in almost complete darkness, surrounded by wilderness, the moon obscured by cloud cover. We pulled off on the left side of the road facing the oncoming traffic, because the shoulder on the right side was practically non-existent.

It was about 30° outside, so I bundled up and got ready to step out into the road. I saw headlights coming toward us in the distance, so I walked twenty or thirty yards in front of the Iveco and waited for those headlights to become a vehicle that I could flag down. When ten minutes or more had passed, the headlights were still a long way off, even though they were still moving toward us. We were on an incredibly straight and flat piece of road.

I began thinking about the seven others and my dog in the truck with no heat, probably needing to use a rest room. Then, before much longer, a car slowly came to a stop where I was standing, and the front passenger window rolled down, revealing a car full of passengers, an entire family of all ages, traveling through the Yukon at three in the morning. "Good evening, folks!" I said, and then quickly explained our plight to them. "I was wondering if you could find it in your hearts to turn around and drive me thirty miles back to that little town and drop me off so that I can find some fuel."

"There is nothing back there," the driver said, "and even if you did find something, everyone is asleep." "Oh, don't you worry about that," I said, "I'll go bang on some doors and get some help... if you'll just take me back there. Please, sir!" "We can't do it," he said.

"Please, sir," I insisted, "I beg of you. I've got seven people in that truck with no heat, and they're going to freeze to death. I'll give you $100 if you do it."

After a moment, the window rolled back up and the folks in the car had a short discussion. The window rolled back down again, and a passenger said, "We just can't do it."

"I'm begging you sir," I lamented. "I'll give you $200."

The window rolled back up. Fifteen seconds later, it rolled down for the last time. "We just can't do it. Good luck to you," said the driver, as he pulled away.

Far off in the distance, I could see another pair of headlights heading our way, so I headed back to the Iveco to tell the group what had transpired and to wait, as I knew it would be another ten minutes or more before the vehicle got to us. Finally, I stepped out of the truck again and walked down the road a bit. A large eighteen-wheeler approached us, and I started to get just a little excited because it appeared to be a fuel tanker! I waved him to a stop and ran around to the driver's door.

"What seems to be the problem here?" he said from beneath his beat-up baseball cap. The man was pure trucker, from his red and black plaid shirt to the five-day salt and pepper stubble that covered his cheeks and chin.

"Well, sir!" I exclaimed. "You are a sight for sore eyes! We ran out of fuel about a half hour ago, and we're just stranded out here with no heat. We've got to be in Fairbanks by daybreak!"

"Oh, man!" he said. "I don't think I can help you. All I've got in here is diesel fuel."

"BUT WE HAVE A DIESEL TRUCK!" I said excitedly.

"Well! Why didn't you say so?" he answered. "I'll get you fixed right up!"

A group photo at the 2006 Young American Showcase Reunion

With that, he jumped out of the cab of his truck and quickly rustled up a fat, yellow hose that he attached to a valve on the side of the tanker. He then stretched out the other end of the hose over to our fuel tank and clamped it onto the wide opening. Without another word, he walked back to the tanker and pulled a lever, filling our fifty-gallon tank in less than a minute.

Pushing the lever back up he said, "You're full!"

"Sir, I cannot thank you enough," I said. "You have saved us from a terrible time and from having to cancel our shows in Fairbanks tomorrow. How much do we owe you?" "Nothing," he said. "They'll never miss that little bit, so don't worry about it."

"Please, sir," I said, "I have to do something for you. Here's $100 for your effort."

"I don't want it," he replied.

"I'd feel much better if you let us show you our appreciation for what you've done," I insisted.

With a heavy sigh, he said, "Well then ... I'll give it to my church."

At that moment, it occurred to me that the Lord had sent one of His own to our rescue. "YES!" I shouted, "GOOD ANSWER!" And I followed this with a hearty, "GOD BLESS YOU!"

He smiled and tipped his cap, before rolling up his window and beginning to slowly creep down the road and into the black night.

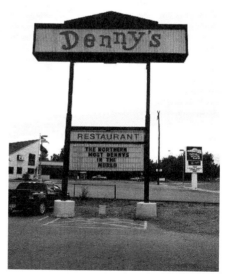

Although it took Stan another thirty minutes and huge blisters on his fingers to prime the bone-dry engine before it would turn over, the band members felt incredibly blessed to be on their way after such a long trip. They even made it to Fairbanks in time to eat breakfast at the "Northernmost Denny's in the World" before having to go do the show. When all was said and done, they knew that it had been one of those times when God asks that you put your faith on the line and walk the walk, believing that He will provide. This became an inspirational story that Stan has told many times through the years, whenever someone wanted to hear a story from the road. Stan says, "God truly is good all the time, if we'll just allow His love to cover us in the worst of times."

Each band had an advance man called a booker, who booked the shows. Stan's story was told at a Showcase reunion in 2007, and the booker who had arranged for the Fairbanks show, a fellow named Bob Miller, was there listening. Bob was a faithful friend who had been with me almost from the very beginning of Showcase. After the reunion, Bob wrote me this letter:

Dear Lowell,

I want to tell you my reaction to the story that Stan told us about what happened twenty-five years ago. I had never heard that story before. The full impact of it didn't hit me until I was on the plane headed home several days later. I still believe I was the only booker ever bold enough (OR STUPID ENOUGH) to have booked dates in "Seward's Folly."

Fairbanks had only two high schools, but after that show, one of them produced the strongest testimonial letter we ever received before or after. It was penned by an 18-year-old young man approximately nine months after that most important evening concert, a concert made possible by the events on that overnight trip and, therefore, an indispensable miracle in our God's plan that directly led to this young man's introduction to and acceptance of a personal relationship with Jesus. Both Fairbanks high schools were on an extremely tight schedule, and the morning assembly for that next morning had no room to be rescheduled. Had they missed that 8:30 a.m. show, one of those high schools, and this young man in particular, would have missed the opportunity entirely. The contents of that letter were heart-stopping.

The young man said that this particular Friday night was to be his first and last concert on this earth. Things were so bad in his life that he took the extraordinary step of putting only two and a half gallons of gas into his truck, carefully picking out the tree he planned to hit on his way home after the concert. Then he heard a sleep-starved young man, not much older than he was, tell him, not about religion, but about a relationship that was the most important thing in the lives of the group. The offer was made to talk to the students after the concert if they had any questions. Boy, did he!

He wrote to us to let us know of the change that evening had made in his life. With his hope restored, he made plans for his future. The day he wrote us, he had just received his acceptance to the state teachers' university in Anchorage. His goal was to become a trained counselor, to help other high school kids. He just wanted us to know and to say, "Thanks."

That letter was the first testimonial that every principal saw on my calls until our ministry finally came to an end. Sure, there were six to eight other letters from administrators and other young people right behind this one, but it was the only testimonial that almost every principal read to the very end.

Due to the real sacrifice of a faithful bunch of people, the intervention of the good Lord himself, and the way-out thinking (literally) of a crazy booker, what a harvest God had in mind! It began with one desperate young guy who met his Master that night, and then continued with every school we were able to book because of his letter, which was largely responsible for the Gospel being brought to thousands and thousands of other young people, many of whom were in circumstances similar to his. Who knows how many young people have found their own pathway to peace from that one soul?

—Bob

I sometimes wonder if Stan was actually speaking with a diesel fuel truck driver from another world. Do angels need an Alaska driver's license?

Ron and Vi Lentini, two other wonderful people who had been in Showcase almost from the beginning, wrote me a little note:

> *As manager, in school after school, I had kids coming up to me asking about the original guys they had seen three years before. Every kid remembered the show and especially the guy's testimony from the night show. Almost everyone had a story about how that night and that show had a major impact on their lives. That's when I realized that there will be several hundred thousand souls in Heaven as a result of this work.*
>
> *— Ron*

CAPTAIN'S LOG:
NEVER GIVE UP!

Dateline: Spring 2000 - ORLANDO, FLORIDA

One of the members of the development group working together on the *Titanic* museum project in Orlando was Michael Harris. I had worked for Mike for a couple of summers, not just in my role as the captain, but also helping sculpt some of the effects in the museum, particularly along the grand staircase, a prominent feature. Now, he had moved into the position of Chief Operating Officer for RMS *Titanic*, the company that owned the salvage rights for diving to the wreck site of the *Titanic*. When I heard that RMS had decided to make another dive in 2000, I thought to myself, "Wouldn't it be neat to actually go down and see the *Titanic* with my own eyes!" I knew my chances were slim, but I had worked for Harris for a couple of years. Maybe, just maybe, he would give me a shot at it. I got up enough courage and called him. But his answer was "No."

Mike was accustomed to such requests. He had people calling him constantly with the same wish. This was the hottest ticket in the world, and he was the only one who could grant permission for the expedition. But every trip the company made to the site of the *Titanic* cost well over $200,000, and on any given venture, the number of trips the submersible might make to the ocean floor depended on the rapidly changing weather conditions. They could sometimes make the fifteen-hour trip to the site with the ship and not be able to make a single dive.

These dives were also very dangerous. It is no small feat to take a small submersible more than two miles below the surface of the unforgiving waters of the North Atlantic, to a wreck that becomes more and more unstable every day. The slightest miscalculation could be disastrous. With room for only three people in the sub each trip, including the captain, Mike had to be strategic about who he let dive. Considering all of this, it was very easy for him to say "no."

I waited two weeks and then called him again. "Mike," I began, "I'm the Captain of the *Titanic*. I think it would be nice if you would let me go."

"No," he said, "that's for archaeologists and important people." The only solace I had in that moment was thinking that at least Barbara thought I was important. There is a legend about a speech Winston Churchill made after World War II. Although the exact facts behind this speech credited to him are fuzzy, the inspiration was crystal clear. The legend goes like this:

After the war was over, Churchill was invited to speak at Harvard University. The professors told the students to have their pads and pens ready, because when this man spoke, it was wisdom. The day came and the old man hobbled up to the microphone and said, 'NEVER GIVE UP! NEVER ... NEVER ... NEVER... GIVE UP!' Then he turned around and sat down.

That was it. That was the whole speech, and I never forgot it.

With Churchill's legend in mind, I mustered up my courage and called Mike again. "Mike, I'm the Captain of the *Titanic*. I'm in front of the camera. I'm in everyone's home. I believe that if the media could say that I've been down to the wreckage site, more people would be interested in hearing what I have to say about your exhibit, and you'll get more people there and, consequently, make more money!"

It got quiet on the other end of the phone, and then Mike said, "I think you're right. Come along." How unbelievable!

Now that I had permission, I SUDDENLY WASN'T SURE I WANTED TO GO! What had I been thinking? I, Lowell Lytle, would be in a Russian submersible going down two and a half miles to the ocean floor! If that wasn't enough to frighten you, I don't know what would.

Mike continued, "Oh, and if you get claustrophobia, forget it.

... And you'll need to get a letter from your doctor saying that you're not going to have a heart attack down there, because we will not be coming back until the dive is over. You will also need to fill out your last will and testament, along with giving your wife power of attorney."

After giving me a few more terrifying instructions, Mike hung up the phone. His assistant just stared at him, incredulous. "What did you just do?" he complained. "You know how many people we have wanting to go down!"

When Barbara and I had a chance to talk it over, I said to her, "I don't know, honey, if I should go after all. It could be very dangerous."

She said, "GO!" I'm not sure what that meant.

Barbara said later that of all of the dangerous situations I had been in over the years, the dive to the *Titanic* frightened her more than anything. For my part, I thought to myself, "I've lived a long time, and if something happens to me on this dive, I know where I'll be going. If I come back safely, I will have an amazing memory of the experience for the rest of my life. It's a win-win situation." So I made the decision to go.

CHAPTER 19

GRIZZLY GREASE

The work in the Young American Showcase ministry was grueling, but exciting. Whenever possible, if a day or two could be spared to enjoy the beauty and variety of our great country, we tried not to miss it. This wasn't always such a good idea.

During one of our critiquing trips, a fellow named Brent Woody and I were traveling out West to critique a band somewhere near the Yellowstone National Park. We had some extra time on our hands, and being near one of the most beautiful parks in America, we made plans to camp overnight somewhere in the mountains. Someone had loaned us a tent and all the paraphernalia that went along with it, so just south of a little town that was at the gateway to Yellowstone, we drove up a mountain road looking for a level spot where we could pitch the tent.

We drove all around and (thankfully) could not find a level spot, so we drove back down the mountain road to a little town, stopping at a small grocery store to ask if anyone knew of a level spot somewhere where we could pitch our tent overnight. The people in the store said, "Are you crazy? There are grizzly bears out there! Nobody camps in tents out here!"

"Okay, that takes care of the camping," we realized. "Do you know of a cabin nearby that might have a fireplace?" If we couldn't have a campfire, at least we could have a fire in the fireplace. The shopkeeper pointed us to a spot about two blocks away where there were some nice log cabins, complete with fireplaces.

We bought a couple of steaks, some bread and other goodies, along with some candles for atmosphere, and headed for the cabins, glad they had a vacancy. There was a portable barbecue grill available, so we cooked our steaks outside, then started a fire in the fireplace, lit the candles and placed them around the room, turning out all the electric lights and enjoying "roughing it."

It was about dusk when we finished eating our steaks. We were talking about how great it would be if we could see a grizzly bear, when I got an idea ... , a horrible ... , distasteful ... , disrespectful ... , beautiful idea! What if we took some of the fat that was left over from the steaks and rubbed it on the wood around the outside of that log cabin, to leave a scent to attract a bear? Brent wanted nothing to do with this scheme, but I got a big handful of that steak fat and managed to give the cabin a pretty good rub down.

Sometime in the middle of the night we heard a "CRASH! BANG! BOOM!" Brent was sleeping next to the window. He looked out and said, "There's a bear out there! And it's dragging our portable barbecue grill away!" The next morning, when we checked out, the owner of the cabin said, "I see that a bear came down to visit you last night. I'm sorry about that. It's the first time a bear has come down here in a long time." Hmmm! I wonder why?

There are no wild grizzlies in Kansas that I know of, but God sure did put some grizzly grease on the Holy Spirit's wheels over the years when Showcase was there. That same year, I arrived to critique the shows in Kansas. While the band manager was inside meeting with the principal, I waited outside with the band and the truck. We had backed up to the gymnasium, where we normally emptied our equipment. As soon as we stopped, I heard a loud bang on the door. As the fellows were jumping out, getting ready to unload, I slid the door open, and a young man asked, "Where is your manager?"

I stepped out and asked, "Can I help you?" He proceeded to tell me this story:

Two years ago, you sent a group through here, and my buddy and I were on the stage crew. There were about eight hundred kids there that night, but he and I were the only Christians in the whole school. About halfway through the evening show, the band stopped and gave their testimony and the plan of salvation—which totally freaked us out. We couldn't believe that anyone would be so bold.

I didn't want anyone to know that I was a Christian, but to hear those fellows come out and be so open with their belief in Christ just blew our minds.

After we packed up your truck that night, the two of us just stood there and watched the team leaving. Their work looked to us like "Mission Impossible." When they had gone, we looked at each other and said, "Man, if they can be so open about their salvation, it's time the two of us do the same."

There was one teacher in the school who was a Christian, and that was it. We asked her if we could have a Bible club in her classroom after school, and she said we could. That was two years ago. Now, eighty percent of the students in the school are born-again Christians, as are the principal, the gym teacher, and all those guys unloading the truck right now. That's the football team.

They were all wearing Fellowship of Christian Athletes T-shirts. I don't remember what particular band it was that did the show he was referring to, but the Lord keeps the books, and there are still ripples going out, many years after those team members did their best that night to communicate the Gospel. Before the assembly program that day, this young man gathered the football team around in a circle and asked me to lead them in prayer. Now, that is "fishing where the fish are!"

Chapter 20

Checkers

Being president of an organization isn't as glamorous as it sounds. Sometimes, the best thing a president can do is pick up a broom and start pushing it. The managers were working hard with their groups around the country, and often my time was best spent taking care of everything needed behind the scenes to keep things running.

I was in Texas one Sunday morning on just such an expedition, trying to buy a pickup truck that would pull a fifth wheeler. It had to be large, and it had to be blue to match the camper I was picking up for one of my managers. I drove to the Dodge dealership at around 1 o'clock in the afternoon, accompanied by Phil Hardly, our spiritual advisor at the time, and also with our Texas advance man, the person responsible for booking shows and taking care of the details before the performances.

When we got to the dealership, we didn't see much activity. I noticed that the front door was open, so we went inside. I didn't see any salespeople, only the cleaning lady. I said to her, "Where are the salesmen?"

She replied, "We're closed on Sunday!"

"Oh," I thought to myself, "that's just great!" I had to be in Colorado the next morning, so this was the only day I had free to buy a truck. I decided that, since I was already on the sales floor, I might as well look around.

I began checking the area to see if I could find the phone number of a salesman who might be interested in coming out on his day off for a guaranteed sale. I noticed eight names on a chalkboard that seemed to be the names of salesmen, and there were phone numbers after them. Each man had a mark next to his name, no doubt indicating how many sales he'd had the previous week. The man next to the bottom only had one mark, so I figured he might be hungry for a sale.

I called the man and told him what I wanted to do.

"Who are you?" he asked.

I repeated my name: "I'm Lowell Lytle."

I went on. "I'm from St. Petersburg, Florida, and I'm here today to buy a pickup truck. If you have the right color, I'll pay you $100 over invoice."

"We're closed today!" he answered, clearly annoyed. "Not only that, but how did you get my number?"

"I saw your name and number here in the office," I said.

"You're in the office?" he asked. Then he paused, thinking, before continuing, "How did you get in there?"

"The door was open," I said, "and the cleaning lady was in here working today." Now I was getting a little annoyed.

"You'll have to come back tomorrow when we're open!" he said.

I was quickly losing my patience. "I won't be here tomorrow," I told him. "I'll be in Colorado in the morning. Today is the only day I have to buy this truck, so if you want to make a hundred dollars over invoice, come over right away, and we will make the deal!"

He grumbled a little bit and then slowly said, "All right … I'll come over."

"What's the matter with this guy?" I thought to myself. "He obviously needs the sale, but he's probably too lazy to leave his televised football game to make $100. No wonder his name was on the bottom of the list."

The three of us went outside and sat in our car and waited about twenty minutes for him to show up. As soon as he pulled up, we got out of our car and walked inside the showroom. Still, the salesman sat in his car a long while… before slowly (and I do mean slowly) shuffling through the door. He looked at us with a nasty look on his face. "Okay, what do you want?"

Now I was really irritated. "Where are your trucks?" I asked.

He pointed to the back door and said, "They're out there." I couldn't believe it. He didn't even come with us. "What a jerk of a salesman," I thought.

We wandered through rows and rows of trucks, but we couldn't find a blue one. About fifteen minutes into our search, the salesman finally came out and slowly worked his way over to me. Looking me right in the face for the first time, he asked, "Are you really here to buy a truck?"

"Yes, of course!" I said.

He breathed a great sigh of relief, mopping his brow and shaking his head. "I thought you were CHECKERS!"

"Checkers?" I thought. "What in the world is he talking about?" I was very confused.

He continued, "Your voice sounds just like him! I've had no sleep in three years. I knew this day would come sooner or later, and when you said this was the only day you could buy, I figured I better come to see you, or you would come over to my place and end it."

"END WHAT?" I thought. He paused, reached down, and slowly raised his sweater to reveal a pistol that held nine bullets.

"So, I came prepared!" he said. "I CAME HERE TODAY TO KILL YOU!"

Needless to say, my heart began to pound. This was not a movie. This was the real thing, and I was the intended target.

Who was this guy? Was he with the Mafia? Who did he think I was? It became immediately obvious that this man was an emotional basket case.

While we began to look for a way out, he proceeded to take us to an old car that he had used for target practice. There were bullet holes all over it.

The poor guy didn't tell us all of the problems that he had gotten himself into, but it was obvious that God had made an appointment for us to meet with him that day. My booker immediately pulled out his pocket-sized New Testament and confronted the salesman with the basic truth: "You need real peace."

I agreed and said to the man, "Let's go into your office and talk." When we all got back to the office and sat down, I said, "I thought we came here today to buy a truck, but that obviously was not the case. God sent us here for a more important reason, and that was to show you how you can have REAL peace!" I took that little New Testament, opened it up to the book of Romans, and shared the path to that peace with the man there in his office. Just a few moments later, he bowed his head, asking Jesus to be his Lord and Savior.

Afterward, you could see the change in him immediately. As true peace spread across his face and throughout his body, he expressed to us that a great burden had been lifted off of his shoulders. Our advance man lived in the same town as this fellow and immediately called his pastor to set up a follow-up program for him.

When we got back in the car, Phil Hardly said to me, "That was amazing. They taught us in Bible school how to lead someone to the Lord, the 1-2-3's of it, but it never seems to work out that way. Today, it surely did."

I could never have planned those events. I went there to buy a blue truck. A man I had never met came prepared to kill me but left with his burdens lifted and his eternal life assured. No one knows what ever happened to "Checkers."

CAPTAIN'S LOG:
DOWN IN THE MORNING

Dateline: August 17, 2000 - ATLANTIC OCEAN
latitude 41° 43' 57" North, longitude 49° 56' 49" West

Less than two weeks before the *Titanic* dive trip, I went up to Clearwater, Florida, to visit a friend of mine, Roger Bansemer. As noted in the early section "About the Cover," Roger is a talented artist and poet, nationally recognized for his artwork and his PBS series, *Painting and Travel with Roger and Sarah Bansemer*. It dawned on me during that visit that perhaps Mike Harris would want an artist along to help record the dive. Here is Roger's account of what happened next:

Roger Bansemer's depiction of my fateful visit in early August of 2000

A large, stout man by the name of Lowell Lytle dropped by my house for a visit, as he often does. He had been a good friend of mine and my family since I was a small boy.

After saying hello, Lowell sank into a chair, but I could tell his enthusiasm level was high. His large hands opened, and with a grand gesture, he announced that he had been invited as a guest to dive to the Titanic. The salvage company that helped to supply artifacts for Titanic exhibitions thought it would be helpful to Lowell's performances for him to actually experience a dive. I sat there in envy and amazement. Just to know someone about to dive to the Titanic was sort of like meeting an astronaut.

As Lowell left my studio, I gave him a copy of my lighthouse book. He told me he would show it to those in charge of the expedition and talk to them about the possibility of my going on the dive, too. "Fat chance," I thought, but it did stir my imagination for the rest of the morning. With book in hand, Lowell drove off to meet with then-Vice President and Chief Operations Officer Mike Harris. My book apparently stirred his imagination, because that afternoon, at about 3 o'clock, the phone rang, and Lowell Lytle was on the other end. "You're invited to go on the expedition" were the words that echoed in my ear. Had Lowell not thought to drop by that morning or had I not been there when he did, things would have been quite different in my life.

Bringing my book to show the expedition leaders opened the way for him to suggest that they consider bringing an artist along. I happened to be in the right place at the right time. After Lowell's convincing pitch, Mr. Harris agreed that they had enough scientists and technicians on the expedition and needed an "artist and a poet" for another view of things. For the rest of the day, I was in shock and disbelief. I had just been given a first-class ticket to the Titanic and had ten days in which to ready myself—both mentally and with supplies.[9]

Roger and I both packed our bags and, just ten days later, flew up to St. John's, Newfoundland, to board the boat that would take us out to the *Akademik Keldysh*, the Russian dive ship and research vessel from which the submersible would be launched at the salvage site. The location of the *Titanic* is 365 miles SSE of St. John's, a journey of a day and a half.

When we arrived in St. John's, we were told that a hurricane was moving over the site, forcing the *Keldysh* to move a hundred miles away until it passed. We would have to stay in St. John's for at least three more days.

Hurricanes and delays were foreboding enough, but then I learned there were going to be twice as many people on that ship as could dive—all hoping for their turn to go down.

Each day that went by, my chances of actually descending to the ocean floor were dropping. After all, Mike hadn't promised

Clowning around overlooking St. John's Bay[11]

me that I would actually dive. He just said I could "come along." Well, there was nothing I could do about it one way or the other. At least, I would be able to be on the water over the site of the *Titanic*. St. John's is a quaint little town filled with very old houses and small, winding streets. It is very picturesque, but you can see it all in about ten minutes. Roger, being the artist he is, was much more taken with the place than was I. I had to look for other ways to amuse myself.

With three days to kill, I thought I'd go see a movie, but I picked the wrong movie to see. It was **THE PERFECT STORM,** the true account of the sinking of the *Andrea Gail,* a disaster that had occurred just nine years earlier! On our way to the site of the *Titanic,* we would have to go over the Grand Banks, the same place where they had filmed the movie, another reason for foreboding.

The Akademik Keldysh [10]

We finally left St. John's and arrived at the Russian research vessel after about a thirty-five-hour journey. Wow, what a massive ship the *Akademik Keldysh* was! It's almost half the size of the *Titanic* but is considered to be the world's largest research vessel. As soon as I had set my belongings on my bunk, I found my way down to see the submersibles.

At the time of this writing, there are only five submersibles in the world that can dive to the depth of two and a half miles. The Americans, Japanese, and French each have one, and

My bunk aboard the Keldysh

the Russians have two: *MIR-1* and *MIR-2*. The cost of each submersible, at that time, was US $20 million. That sounded good to me! It gave me confidence that they were built properly... until I got close enough to inspect one of them and found that it had been repaired with DUCT TAPE! I guess if duct tape is good enough for outer space, then it's good enough for twelve thousand, five hundred feet below sea level. Still, I started doubting myself. Did I really want to do this?

Later we walked around, meeting some of the important people I had been told would be there. Some of them had climbed to the top of Mount Everest; some were extremely wealthy. Most likely, none of them drove a fifteen-year-old car, like I did.

One of the first things on our agenda was to have a briefing in the conference room on what would be expected of us if we were chosen to dive. A short time later, someone shouted, "The subs are coming back!" This obviously was a big moment, because people ran in every direction to get their cameras to record what was about to happen. Then, everyone gathered on the main deck to get the best possible view. This same scene would take place every night while we were at sea.

Each sub would come to the surface right around sunset. Sometimes it would be totally dark, and from a distance you could see the lights of the sub about a hundred feet under the water, a soft, glowing blue light which would let the crew waiting on the surface in a rubber Zodiac (an inflatable motorized boat) know exactly where it was. When the sub finally surfaced, the cowboys (as we called them) would leap from the Zodiac onto

The MIR ready to be lifted back onto deck[12]

The MIR returns [13]

the sub, sometimes in rough seas, and fasten a tow rope to the front of it.

Once the sub was towed to the side of the *Keldysh*, a large crane would swing out over the water and a cowboy would ride on the back of the sub in order to attach the crane's cable. These men really did look like cowboys trying to ride a horse... while ocean swells did their best to either knock them off of the subs, crash the Zodiacs into them, or lift and tilt the crane hovering overhead until it swept them off or injured them. It was very dangerous work. In the end, the crane slowly lifted the submersible out of the water and gently set it on the deck.

When the hatch cover was opened and the three men inside crawled out, the nearly one hundred people present to see it all began clapping and cheering, as if these men had just come back from the moon. Considering the fact that there have been three times as many people in outer space as have ever seen the *Titanic* at the bottom of the ocean, I suppose this jubilation was justified. I was just happy to see them come back safely from a two-and-a-half-mile dive to the ocean floor.

The dining hall aboard the Akademik Keldysh [28]

While the divers were being interviewed by the television camera team, a work crew came out from the conservator's room and collected all the salvage items picked up on this particular dive. These items were taken into a special room, where they would be scrutinized by a conservator, who was extremely knowledgeable about every piece of the *Titanic*. The items would immediately be categorized and then placed into water to prevent any further deterioration. This routine happened every day. The subs would go down, and then twelve hours later they would come back, and we would all gather in the conservator's room to see what treasures had just been found.

After several days and nights of watching the launch and return of the submersible, I could see that a journey to the bottom of the ocean would not be a pleasure trip. Those men, much younger and more fit than I, returned elated, but exhausted. If I ever did get a chance to go down, would I be able to handle it? Then, one evening while I was eating my dinner, Mike Harris came over to my table, leaned over to me, and said, "You're going down in the morning."

CHAPTER 21

SNUG HARBOR

As the years went by, one of Young American Showcase's biggest problems became our growth. What had started as a single group in 1969 had become two groups by that same winter with the help of my good friend, manager, and faithful booker, Bob Miller. By 1971, we had four groups on the road and had presented the Gospel to over a million high school and middle school students in that year alone. In the summer of that year, we had over forty thousand decisions for Christ.

These new Christians needed follow-up, information about spiritual growth and a way to connect with other Christians, or their newfound faith would quickly falter. We turned to the Billy Graham organization, and, under the leadership of George Wilson, they took care of the entire follow-up ministry. The numbers were overwhelming. Thousands of students were hungry for the Gospel and ready to follow Christ.

As we continued to grow and add groups, follow-up became more and more of an issue. A ministry called "The Way" took over, after the Billy Graham organization, and managed follow up until they, also, could not keep up with the demand. From 1976 to 1992, Young American Showcase had placed as many as eight groups a year throughout the United States and Canada, sending one group as far away as Australia.

Before Showcase, Terry and I had used creativity and ingenuity to build our own drive-in ministries with very little financial support. Within the Showcase ministry, I had many fulfilling opportunities to use my own creative and problem-solving abilities in the shows and, after that, to retrofit trucks, build durable props, and figure out how to make it all work. But, at this point, most of the work Barb and I were doing was in leadership. Things were running smoothly, and the company had grown about as far as it could. Should we expand, start more groups, or start something brand new? How could I put the creative ability God had given me to use? We now had a unique inroad with junior high and high schools, but what about elementary school children?

As we approached the mid 1970s, we had long ago outgrown our kitchen table, and then the carport. Barb was still managing the books, juggling children's schedules, and keeping the administration of the business going, but when even the carport couldn't hold it all, we finally decided we needed an office.

I went to see a realtor, telling him what we needed, and that I would love to see a piece of property on the water. "It's too bad you weren't here two months ago," he said. "I sold a piece of property that would have been ideal for you."

"Where is that property?" I asked, my curiosity growing. "Snug Harbor," he said.

I had to see what I missed.

When I arrived at the Snug Harbor property, I couldn't help but notice that it was off the beaten path. I parked the car and started walking down a little pathway that led alongside a single-level motel that had been built on the property years before. There were beautiful flowering bushes to my left and right.

Past a shuffleboard court, there was a large hibiscus bush that had grown into a tree. This seemed strange to me. In 1962, a devastating hard freeze had killed most of the vegetation in Pinellas County. Because I had worked in landscaping to help support the family during the lean times and had become particularly taken with tropical vegetation, especially palm trees, I had planted a beautiful palm at the Florida drive-in, and carefully nurtured another one I had planted in front of our own home. That is until the freeze of 1962 killed it. Somehow, this little plot of ground had not been harmed.

I spotted a massive bright red bougainvillea growing to my left, and

Snug Harbor

then, as I walked further down the pathway, I saw an actual bayou. There were mangroves and an island on the other side of the glistening water.

I picked up the pace, anxious to see what other wonders lay before me. And then, what was this? Four large coconut palms leaned out over the water. I couldn't believe it. There is no tree as dramatic as the coconut palm, and I like to think that it was the last thing God created before He rested.

Suddenly my imagination had taken over, just as on that day so long ago when, in childhood, I had opened the door of that barn on Clinton Street for the first time. I thought to myself, "What could I do with this?" It looked like paradise.

The lady who now owned the property was out mowing the grass. I said, "Hello, I would like to buy this piece of land."

"It's not for sale!" she said.

But something I had practiced all my life and passed on to all the young men and women of Showcase was tenacity. "Never take 'NO' for an answer," I had taught them. "Never let an obstacle keep you from going where God wants you to go." Around Showcase, this became known as the make-it-happen doctrine, and now I was determined to make this sale at Snug Harbor happen. That lady and her husband had no idea that they had bought that property just so we could buy it from them two months later, but that's what we did.

We were now the owners of a motel with an adjoining house on the waterfront at Snug Harbor, and it was this house which became the office for Young American Showcase. Not only could we fulfill our office space needs, but we could hire more people to help us and also rent rooms out to help with expenses!

It was a beautiful location. There were no buildings across the water from us, only some uninhabited islands. The view out into the harbor was very tropical, remote, and inviting. Our son, David, was particularly taken by it, spending hours and hours, day after day rowing out to the islands, imagining a pirate's life, exploring, and running into all sorts of creatures of the bayou.

Not far from Snug Harbor, at the pier in St. Petersburg, the *Bounty*, a replica of the 1787 Royal Navy ship built in 1960 for MGM's *Mutiny on the Bounty*, was berthed. She had spent her winters there since the movie's debut in 1962, and we had been aboard the *Bounty* often, admiring her beautiful lines. I had gotten to know her captain and crew, fascinated by her history and the romance surrounding this famous sailing ship.

David, too, was captivated by it all, and when he asked me to make his bedroom look like an old ship, I gladly fulfilled his request, happy to have a creative outlet. The walls of his room were planked, his bed was placed on a

dock, and there was a mast with sails and a wooden ship's wheel, along with a real ship's hatch cover for a desk. He loved it!

We knew it was time for Young American Showcase to think bigger as well. In just under three years, our country would be celebrating its Bicentennial. We already had plans to create a new morning show, emphasizing a patriotic theme, to perform at schools and were going to call those groups "Freedom Jam." They would use the same format – high energy, entertaining day shows at junior high and high schools to draw interest and then rock n' roll shows at night with a Gospel message delivered at the end. We were also planning a version of those shows for general audiences, a choral musical group with different genres of music, representing two hundred years of American songs, to be performed in auditoriums around the country.

First, we needed a brochure, and we thought the *Bounty* would make a fine backdrop for our photo shoot. We took several shots aboard the ship, in full costume.

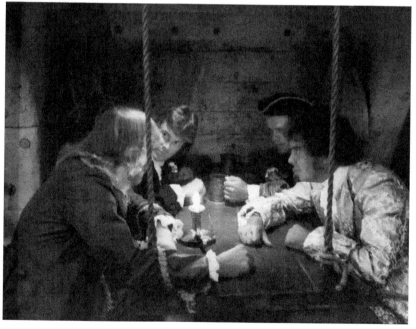

In the hold of the Bounty
(From left to right) Wayne Hackett, myself, Ray Nicolas, and Joe Lathrop

No matter how big your dreams may be, God's dreams for you are always bigger. Don't be afraid to sail out into high seas before you have the entire map before you. If God says, "MOVE," you'd better start moving.

With a dock and a beautiful bayou at our doorstep and with Showcase running smoothly, our family began to talk about purchasing a houseboat to take out on the water for recreation. My good friend, Joe Lathrop, said to me, "I'm surprised at you, Lowell. You're more creative than to buy a plastic boat! It seems like you would build something."

I thought to myself, "Maybe he's right." With David's interest in old ships and my newfound interest in possibly building one, I proceeded to the local hobby shop to look for inspiration, and picked up some drawings I found of the *Santa Maria*. On the dining room table, with

13-year-old David and our 15-year-old neighbor, Mark Lach, looking over my shoulder, I made some calculations as to the size the vessel would need to be. Barbara was in the kitchen, doing dishes, and she began shaking her head and thinking, "Oh, no, there goes my house boat."

In costume at the helm of the Bounty

But wouldn't it be fun to tool around the harbor in a houseboat made to look like the *Santa Maria*? That was my plan, but, as usual, God's plans were far greater than mine. I was about to step into an adventure that would take me far closer to the bottom of the ocean than I ever thought I wanted to be.

CHAPTER 22

THE *SANTA MARIA*

We were going to build a boat for a family project, and that's as far as our plans went. It would turn out to be a risky and expensive decision, and at the time, I had no idea just how dangerous it would also turn out to be. Had I known, I might have stuck with a simple houseboat!

Remember, at Young American Showcase, we had been thinking about how to expand our reach from junior and senior high school youth to include elementary school children. While we were preparing for the upcoming Bicentennial celebrations and working on the script for the patriotic shows we wanted to do, the connection came to us. A floating *Santa Maria* could be used for elementary school field trip exhibits around the country, so the shipbuilding project became part of the Young American Showcase ministry. Barb was right: so much for a family houseboat!

Of course, I knew nothing about boats, let alone designing them, so I found a boat designer in Halifax, Nova Scotia, by the name of James (Doug) Rosborough. He gave us instructions on what kind of wood we needed and how long it should be stacked to dry out, which was right around six months. He also said, "See if you can find an old-time boat builder down there who knows how to build wooden ships." We stacked the wood, found a boat builder, and a few months later, after many long-distance discussions, Doug sent down the plans for a sixty- eight-foot-long replica of the *Santa Maria*. His description of the project from his book, *Confessions of a Boatbuilder*, can give you a sense of the intricacy and difficulty of planning and building what would become literally a beautiful floating museum:

Lowell and his partner, Joe Lathrop, set to willfully and laid her keel in the small community of Snug Harbor, Florida, in May 1974. John Bodden was hired as master carpenter and much amateur help was forthcoming from son, family and friends of [Young American Showcase]. ... Santa Maria's hull took shape and rose higher and higher among the palm trees. Much of her material was of Florida pine and cypress for frame and planking. The long building process continued, as we began to build all her masts, spars and rigging, and the boats at A.F. Theriault's yard in the Meteghan River.

We found antique iron, wooden stock anchors salvaged from old shipwrecks in St. Mary's Bay. We had working iron cannons cast at Lunenburg Foundry, while Theriault's made up the carriages and tackle. Pulley blocks, hearts, trucks, parrel and belaying pins were made to order at Dauphinee's Block Shop in Lunenburg, while all her Dacron, tan-bark sails were provided by the loft of R.B. Stevens & Sons. When all was made ready, we loaded it on a tractor-trailer and shipped it off to Lowell in Florida.[14]

We had done plenty of research on what the interior of the ship would have looked like and did our best to recreate it.

We now notified event planners in New York City that the *Santa Maria* would be sailing into New York Harbor for their Bicentennial Celebration and tall ships parade, known as "Operation Sail," planned to be the largest tall ships parade in a hundred years. At the same time, we were able to convince Christopher Columbus XVIII to come to America and be on the *Santa Maria* when we went up the Hudson River for the water parade into the city that day. I know it sounds funny, but he was the real living descendent of Christopher Columbus and had papers to prove it, so we wanted him on our ship for that historic occasion!

To be ready by July 4th, 1976, we would have to work fast. Like Noah building his ark, Joe Lathrop and I cut, shaved, measured, and fit board after board right by the water at our Snug Harbor location, with a growing crew of volunteer boat builders at our side. No doubt my neighbors, just like Noah's, thought we were crazy!

Meanwhile, during the summer rehearsal camp of 1975, half of our groups prepared to do the new patriotic show. The first show was in Tarpon Springs, Florida, and it was a huge hit.

Now, we just had to get the boat finished. After all the delays and adjustments one runs into on any grand project, the Santa Maria launched into the waters of Snug Harbor in April 1976, and we spent the next two months stepping the mast and finishing all the rigging.

"Stepping" a mast involves setting it down in a hole in the center of the ship. A huge crane is used to lift the mast and slowly lower it, as the crew members guide it through that hole down to the keel, or spine, of the boat, and then secure it by the ratlines that steady the mast to the sides of the ship. We placed a silver dollar under the mast for good luck and safe passage, an ancient nautical tradition. Perhaps that coin would have been better spent elsewhere.

Still, the ship was looking great, and why shouldn't she be? Ray Nicholas, a well-known finish carpenter, had labored tirelessly in the hot Florida sun all that time, proving himself to be one of the finest wooden boat builders around. Then, in the summer of 1976, we launched the Santa Maria, finally commissioned for the sea, her mission one of "Bringing history to life, and life to history!" When I'd started the project, I had no idea how to build a sailing vessel, and yet here she sat, not by my own ability, but by the efforts of a huge team of people and God's faithful blessing.

But, building a square-rigger is not the same as sailing it. We needed a captain. I decided to bring a deep-water sailor by the name of Adrian Small over from England. He had been the first mate on the Mayflower II and had also sailed a little square-rigged ship in the Great Lakes for four years. He had sailed the Golden Hind from England to America the year before, so I hired him and his crew to come and do the honor of sailing the Santa Maria. He had written a book about his previous sailing experiences in which he said, "I wish I'd had wheels on the keel because I put it on the ground so many times." I should have learned from that, because we went aground eleven times before we got to Norfolk, Virginia. The biggest blessing among the British crew was Richard Turnage, who, after the first year, became the first mate.

We left for the tall ships celebration in New York from the St. Petersburg municipal pier, surrounded by more than five hundred small boats. The crew were all dressed in period costumes, which made it ideal for the local television cameramen. It was quite a sight! Everyone was excited! We were on our way to the adventure of a lifetime. We were headed to sea on a square-rigged ship, with a famous deep-water sailor as the captain! What could possibly go wrong?

When Captain Adrian Small had gotten off the plane in Florida, he appeared to be a typical Englishman. He was, for sure, the perfect image of a salty sea captain. He had a red beard, piercing blue eyes, and disheveled clothes, and carried a duffel bag in which he kept all of his belongings. He was an artist who had illustrated two books, which may explain some of the melancholy temperament we were to encounter.

With Captain Adrian Small, discussing the blueprints for the Santa Maria [15]

I should have picked up on a possible conflict when he told a reporter before we set sail, "Handling sailing ships is not that difficult... handling the people is the problem." There were many things he didn't like about the ship or the crew, especially that my son David and Joe Lathrop, Jr., were allowed to come along for the ride. He called them "grommets," which is somewhat demeaning for a sailor. A grommet is a small insignificant ring on the corner of a sail through which a rope is attached. He said, "Those two 17-year-old boys will never make it past Miami." They both made the complete trip.

As we sailed under the Sunshine Skyway Bridge, we fired all four of our cannons, as a salute. The television crew disembarked when we ventured into the Gulf of Mexico. We were on our way.

When the last passenger had left and all of the motorboats had gone, the captain ordered a meeting of all the crew on the main deck. Joe Lathrop looked at me and said, "Oh boy! The captain's going to speak!"

We all gathered in the waste area, which is another term for the main deck, while the captain stood on a ladder between the quarterdeck and the poop deck. The first thing out of his mouth was, "I am appalled at you people. You are not sailors. This ship is not ready to go to sea. The people who just left us drinking their Dr. Peppers and iced tea are going ashore to sleep on dry land. They are called day sailors. We are going to sea on the same ocean and the same kind of a ship Columbus sailed on. This is not a pleasure trip. This is a matter of life and death, and I want you to know that NOBODY DOES ANYTHING ABOARD THIS SHIP UNLESS I TELL YOU!"

When he had finished, Joe looked at me and said, "I thought this was going to be a 'Yo ho ho' trip; instead, it's a 'No no no' trip!"

Captain Small was right about it not being a pleasure trip and that everything we did on the ship could, and would, easily become a matter of life and death. On our first day out, we had to immediately head back to shore in Bradenton, Florida, for some minor repairs.

Our first crewman jumped ship as soon as we landed. The next evening, we were sailing south of Fort Myers when a wind storm blew in. I was in my bunk sleeping at the time, when suddenly I heard the ship's bell ringing continually. I knew that was a call for "all hands on deck!" With no time to get dressed, the only thing we were all wearing was our undershorts.

When I arrived on deck, the scene around me alerted all my senses of the danger. The sails, flapping violently in the wind as the men clewed them up, sounded like machine guns going off! We all ran to our assigned locations and awaited instructions from the captain. The lightning, thunder, and winds were furious. I was concerned about whether the planks might break loose. This was our first storm, and I thought it might be our last! We were all terrified!

My position was the quarter deck, and I was responsible for controlling eight different lines that went to *somewhere*. (I was never quite sure where.) All hell was breaking loose!

The captain stood on the poop deck, giving orders. In between the lightning flashes, I could see him standing there with a pipe in one hand and a cup of tea in the other. I thought, "What's the matter with him? Doesn't he know we might perish?" He took it all in stride, as if everything was under control. I started to feel a little more comfortable about the situation... until he gave a command that had something to do with the lines in front of me. I didn't know which line to pull or release, so I thought, I've got one chance in eight to get it right. I reached for one line, and he shouted, "NO!"

"Oh, that's just great!" I thought. "I'm not only scared to death, but I look like a fool too, and I'm the owner of this vessel!" We made it through the storm, and the captain congratulated the sailors, rewarding them with some rum from the galley.

There was no question about this captain running a tight ship, and I think most everyone was afraid of him. He never ate with us below deck. In fact, he never went below deck unless he was inspecting something. He slept and ate up above in the great cabin. He wouldn't even come down and get his food. Instead, he made the "grommets" carry it up to him. A part of that I didn't like, but another part I did. He was there to lead his men, not to win friends.

We were sailing north in the Atlantic Ocean one balmy evening, with the wind to our back. The sails were full, and we had just finished a wonderful meal that our cook, Joe Lathrop, had fixed for us. We had now all gathered out on the main deck and were looking at the full moon and feeling that wonderful summer breeze on our face, when I said to Adrian, "Isn't this fantastic?"

He said, "The ropes are chafing."

The next night, the same thing happened. I said, "Come on, Adrian, this is wonderful."

His response was, "The wind's in the wrong direction." Somehow, it

The Santa Maria *with her sails full, heading out to sea*

seemed like nothing ever pleased him.

The morning after our first storm, we were motoring south into the wind when our engine faltered, the first sign of many engine troubles to come. We had barely made it around the tip of Florida into the Atlantic Ocean. I ordered another engine to be picked up in Miami.

There we also picked up a new first mate. His name was Fred Quillen, and he had never sailed on a square-rigged ship before. However, he had been a pilot on the Chesapeake Bay for twenty years and knew a lot about motor sailing. His credentials seemed to pass inspection from our captain, so we hired him and brought him on board. He was a softspoken gentleman and not afraid to eat with the boys down below.

CAPTAIN'S LOG: Debris Field

Dateline: August 17, 2000 - ATLANTIC OCEAN
latitude 41° 43' 57" North, longitude 49° 56' 49" West

When I heard those words, "You're going down in the morning," my heart began to pound. "This is it!" I couldn't believe it. I thought, "It's actually going to happen. This isn't a dream; I'm going to be one of the fortunate ones." I don't believe I even finished my meal that evening. That night, while I was lying in bed, my mind was spinning like a top, imagining all the images I might see on the ocean floor.

I'm not sure that I got much sleep at all, but the next morning I got up quite early and went to see the person in charge of my diving suit. When he saw me, he said, "You're too big. You'll never get into that sub."

"I'll make it!" I insisted. I wasn't going to get that far and not at least try to go all the way.

"We don't have a fire suit big enough for you," he told me.

"FIRE SUIT?" I asked. "What's this about a fire?"

"Well, you'll be breathing one hundred percent oxygen, and there's always the possibility of a fire."

"Well, if there is a fire, I would only last ten seconds. What good would the suit be?"

"It's for identification," he said.

"IDENTIFICATION? I'm that tall guy down there!" They gave me the largest suit they had, and I somehow squeezed into it.

From that point on, the television cameraman followed me around like I was an astronaut. I walked by the doorway to the cafeteria and saw the two men who were preparing to dive in

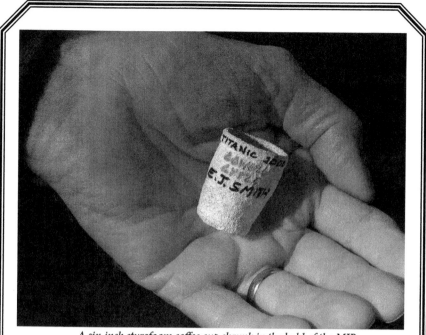

A six-inch styrofoam coffee cup shrunk in the hold of the MIR

the other sub sitting at a table, writing names on a pile of six-ounce styrofoam coffee cups. "What are you doing?" I asked.

"Oh, you need to get some of these," I was told. "You can give them to some of your friends. You can draw pictures or people's names on them, and then they're placed in a bag that is put into the battery section of the sub, exposing them to six thousand pounds of pressure per inch. When they come back, that six-ounce styrofoam coffee cup will be the size of a thimble. Your friends will love it." It sounded like a great idea to me, so I wrote different people's names on some cups to give away as gifts.

After a light breakfast, I went to the submersible operations room to get my final instructions. They wanted us to pick up any coal we found, because they could sell pieces of it at the exhibits, and they also wanted a rectangular first-class window if we could find one. They also let us know, in no uncertain terms, not to pick up a port hole. They already had too many of those. There would be three of us in that submersible, two observers and one Russian pilot.

I had to sign something that listed me as a crew member, and then we continued to prepare. My blood pressure, I'm sure, must have been very high at that point. Every emotion you could think of was going through my body. I hardly registered what was going on around me. Roger Bansemer summed up my feelings very well when he wrote:

> We were finally called to attention and let in on some of the conversation as the head of the Mir Group, Anatoly Sagalevich, spoke in English. I listened intently but didn't hear one single word. My emotions were at such a high pitch that it all went right past me. If he had said the watertight hatch had just been replaced with a new screen door and as soon as we hit the water we would sink like a stone and never come up, I would have just been smiling and nodding my head. OK, let's do it![16]

When the meeting was over, we filed out of the room toward the submersible, but I was halted for a few minutes by Fox News. They wanted an interview before I dove. They wanted to know what I was feeling at that moment. I did my best to answer, but it probably made no sense.

Being interviewed just before the dive

When I finally started to climb onto the sub, someone shouted, "Lowell Lytle, you're the oldest person to ever dive to the *Titanic!*" Great! That was just what I needed to hear!

When I got to the top of the ladder, there was a Russian technician who told me I had to remove my shoes due to the fact that there was probably oil and hydraulic fluid on the bottom of them. Any small amount of fluids picked up while walking on the deck of the ship could mix with the hundred-percent-oxygen atmosphere and cause spontaneous combustion, burning all of us alive. In that moment, I knew what the fire suit was all about.

Boarding the MIR

After removing my shoes and giving a customary wave to those standing around, I slipped through the hatch, trying to be as careful as I could not to tip over any of the instruments. Wouldn't you know it, my long legs just wouldn't cooperate. The first thing I did was kick over an oxygen tank. Boy, you should've seen that Russian pilot come alive!

My first thought was, "Well, that's not a very good omen. I hope it gets better from here." I looked around for a place to sit, only to find that there was only one seat and that belonged to the Russian pilot. The other observer and I had to find comfort on a board that was about three feet long and twelve inches wide. I could sit on my knees, lie on my back with my knees up to my chin, or lie on my side in a fetal position for the next twelve hours. I thought, "This is not going to be comfortable, but I can do this." Anyway, it was too late. They had secured the hatch cover, so I couldn't change my mind if I wanted to.

I crouched on my knees, looking through a four-inch viewport on the side of the *MIR*, until suddenly I felt our sub being lifted off the deck and then being placed in the water. We bobbed around in the water for what seemed to be about ten minutes. Then, the beautiful blue water started turning green, as we began our descent. After fifteen minutes, the water was totally black, and I was alone with my thoughts. I started to think how hot it was in the sub.

It was August, and the sub had been sitting on the deck for quite some time, with the sun beating down on it. And three grown men, all cramped into a six-and-a-half-foot sphere, along with all the instruments, put out an incredible amount of heat. On top of all that, I was wearing long winter underwear.

I had been told that it was going to be cold down there. The water temperature at twelve thousand, five hundred feet below sea level in the summertime is 34°. Inside the sub, it would be around 40° or so. I would basically be sitting inside of a refrigerator for seven hours. But at the moment, it was hot. It must have been 95° in there. I noticed that the other two men had already unzipped their fire suits down to their waists, so I followed suit. The Russian pilot gave me a towel to dry myself off. Not only was I sweating, but condensation sprinkles on you all the time you are in the submersible.

I rolled over on my back, with my knees up to my chin. The other men were quiet. The only thing I could hear was static from a small speaker just above my head, where once in a while, a Russian would be sending some instructions from the *Keldysh*.

There were no lights on inside or out, for they wanted to save the energy in the batteries. The only lights I could see now were the lights of the instrument panels. Other than that, we were in complete darkness. After about an hour, I felt quite comfortable. The water temperature on the outside of the sub had started to cool us down, so we all zipped up our fire suits and settled in for another seventy-five-minute ride to the ocean floor. Even though we were descending at about one hundred feet per minute, there was no feeling of motion at all.

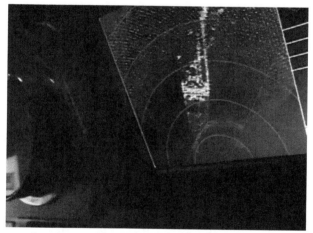

Sonar image of the Titanic from inside the submersible

The anticipation that I was feeling about seeing the *Titanic* was amazing. Then, a few minutes before we arrived at the site, the Russian pilot turned on the outside lights and said, "We're almost there." I quickly turned over and pressed my face against the viewport, only to see something that I didn't want to see. The ocean floor was coming up at us way too fast. We hit it and bounced. I didn't need that!

After about five minutes, the sediment settled, and I could actually see what was on the ocean floor. I felt like I had just

A crab rests on some distress rockets in the Titanic's debris field [17]

landed on some distant planet because the sea life was so very strange. Of course, I could see the *Titanic* debris scattered all around, but what startled me was to see pure white crabs, and starfish about fourteen to fifteen inches in diameter, each finger of the starfish no bigger around than your little finger. They moved across the ocean floor like spiders. I asked the Russian pilot where we were. He said, "We're in the debris field."

"Where are we in relationship to the bow?" I asked.

"If you want to go to the bow, we'll have to go now, because we won't have time to do it later," he responded. So, off we went.

With the outside lights on, you could see approximately fifty feet ahead of you. There is sediment continually falling, but in spite of that, it's quite clear. After a while, you get lulled into feeling that you could actually get out and walk around.

Of course, you would be crushed instantly. Many people ask, "Are there skeletons down there?"

No! The salt water and sea life would have consumed them many years ago.

After about five minutes, I saw a massive black thing in front of me. It was covered with what looked like icicles but was actually rust created by the microorganisms that are eating up the ship. These are known as rusticles. We started to rise, as if we were in an elevator, and pretty soon, THERE IT WAS! THE BOW OF THE *TITANIC*!

A delicate sea plant grows on the very tip of the bow, impervious to water pressure.[19]

CHAPTER 23

MUTINY!

The crew of the *Santa Maria*, working hard to learn as quickly as possible the rules and rhythms of sailing a square-rigger, was also learning the unpredictability of the sea. We had worked our way up the Florida coast past Georgia and were sailing near Myrtle Beach, South Carolina, "the graveyard of the Atlantic," when a nor'easter wind blew down the coast, hitting us head on and churning up waves so high that the froth on the white caps seemed to float off into the air. The ship was pitching violently, to the point that the ship's bell was ringing on its own. The sails were trimmed and tied down, useless in the storm, leaving us dependent on only our engine to push us through the gigantic waves. The men below deck trying to sleep had to be tied in their bunks, and we were not making any headway.

Around three o'clock in the morning, the engineer came to my bunk and said, "Lowell, the sea has opened up the planks, and we are taking on water. The sawdust that never got removed from the bilge has clogged up our pumps! The only pump that is still working is the one on the main engine, and it's sucking air from the fuel line. They are forcing fuel into the engine by using a pop bottle. Our batteries are so weak that if the engine stops, we'll never get it started again. Our radio can only transmit about a hundred yards. I haven't had sleep in three days, and I want off at the next port!"

Well, after all of that information, I was just glad to hear him say something about a "next port." I said, "No, from here on you and your dog get a free ride. You've worked hard enough, but you need to see the tall ships parade. I'll find another engineer—if we ever get to shore.

In the meantime, open up the main hatch and give everyone a bucket. I'm not going down without a fight!"

I climbed out of my bunk and went to the engine room and, sure enough, there were three men huddled around the engine, pouring fuel into it with a pop bottle. The engine was making pulsating sounds, as if it were trying to stop and then start again. I went to the galley, picked up a soup strainer, and headed for the bilge.

The bilge is the lowest part of a ship, the space between the lowest deck and the angled bottom of the ship, where the two rounded sides join. If the bilge compartments flood, the ship cannot stay afloat. Now, I'm 6' 4", and I found it very difficult to crawl down into the bilge, which was only three and a half feet high.

That wasn't the only problem; the ocean was now inside of the ship, and every time the ship rocked, I was slammed up against the ribs of the ship, back and forth. I tried my best to use the soup strainer to keep the wood chips from clogging up the main engine pump, all the while fighting off cramps in my legs.

The crew was not happy with the captain and probably hated me, because I had built the ship. I know they were frightened, exhausted, and being pummeled by the storm as they worked. There were so many ways this could end; the worst was certainly a strong possibility, but in moments like this, you can't think about the worst. You can only pick up a bucket, or a soda bottle, or a soup strainer, and get to work!

I would reflect back on the danger of this situation thirty-six years later, when I watched the HMS *Bounty*, whose wheel I'd had the privilege of taking, and whose captain I counted as a friend, slip below the ocean's surface, as the full fury of Hurricane Sandy boiled above her. The HMS *Bounty* began taking on water, and her bilge pumps became clogged, just as ours had. The captain himself worked to free the filters of debris. Once the bilge pumps failed, the water level inside the ship rose... until the engines flooded and quit. Then, the generators gave way. Dead in the water, waves crashing and pouring water into her from above, as the ocean filled up the bowels of the ship, she foundered, and two lives were lost, ultimately due to the captain's decisions (according to the investigation by the NTSB).

Captain Walbridge went down with his ship that day, his body never recovered. I mourned his loss, and was struck by the sinking of such an incredible sailing vessel. How close had we come to the same fate? More than three decades earlier, twisted into a knot in the bowels of my own ship, doing the simplest, yet most difficult of tasks to try to keep the last pump going, fighting to keep her afloat, the last thing I could imagine wanting to repeat would be a predicament like this. Yet, there was to be another such adventurous moment in my life many years later, when I would be crammed into a still smaller space, under water, fighting off cramps in my legs again, staring at the ocean floor.

A large tanker was passing, near enough to pick up our signal. We radioed him about our plight, but there was no way he could help us. He transferred the information to our home office, as the captain somehow managed to turn the ship around, put up the sails, and let the storm carry the *Santa Maria* on the surf back into Charleston, South Carolina.

After licking our wounds, making repairs, and finding a new engineer, we decided to motor up the Intracoastal Waterway for the rest of the trip, a safer route, away from the dangers of the open sea, land within easy reach on either side. We had traveled about a mile or so when we passed a house on the waterfront, to the delight of the owner, who quickly ran in the house, grabbed his camera, and started snapping photos of us hobbling along. I am sure his photos showed an interesting progression, for just two hundred yards farther, our engine failed again.

We lowered the dinghy and motored back to his house to tell him our unbelievable plight; we were on our way to the tall ships parade in New York Harbor, we had to be there by July 4th, we were stranded a mile inland, and we needed a mechanic who could understand the workings of an old, rebuilt diesel engine. Lastly, we had no money. How many places in the world could we find someone who would be willing to help us out of such a mess?

"Yes! I know someone," he said, "a Christian man who's a mechanic!" This man had a reputation for helping people, regardless of their circumstances, and, sure enough, he was willing to help us, too. He came aboard and started tearing the engine apart. I reminded him: "I'm sorry, but I can't pay you now. With all of our expenses, we have no more money." With head and shoulders bent into his work, he answered, "We'll worry about that later. Right now, we have to get you to New York."

A naturally gifted mechanic is priceless and hard to find. He intuitively understands the workings of an engine, the principles of the machinery, whether it's a small toy motor or, in this case, the engine of a large ship. He worked, and we prayed, and soon we were on our way up the ditch again. I paid him a year later.

As if the experience wasn't painful enough up to this point, it kept getting worse! The morale of the crew was very poor. By the time we arrived in Norfolk, Virginia, one man had an appendicitis attack, our cook and a few others quit, even the captain himself quit! We were out of money and almost out of food. Our engineer's constipated dog didn't make our trip any easier. He would not relieve himself on board the ship. We would slide papers under the quarterdeck, hoping that he would do his business on them, but he never did.

After we phoned our office and told them all of our troubles, we set off again up the Chesapeake Bay, still more than three hundred miles from our destination. We had promoted our first mate, Fred Quillen, to captain. The more seasoned sailors on board wondered if he would be any good, but when he backed that ship out of our slip and turned it on a dime, they were all amazed!

We had motored about eight hours up the waterway toward our destination when—in the middle of the night, wouldn't you know it—the engine failed again. Fortunately, the wind was coming from the south, so our sails were full. We sailed all night, until early in the morning.

Captain Quillen, who knew the Chesapeake like the back of his hand, decided to take the ship up a river to a small town called Onancock to get the engine fixed. The river was narrow and winding, and with only our sails to work with, navigating its waters would not be an easy task. Quillen could only use the top sail, for the river was too narrow to use the main yard arm to shift to port or starboard. It had to be braced on an angle so that it would not hit the trees as we went by.

Houses dotted the river, and by the time we approached the main dock, word had spread. It seemed as if the whole town had shown up at the dock to greet us. Thank goodness! We needed all the help we could get.

It's hard to stop a ninety-eight-ton ship with no engine. We put our longboat over the side and tied it to our ship, hoping that the little motor on that boat would help us control our steering. Our amazing captain saw all the people standing on the dock and shouted for them to help fend off, and they did! We came right up to the dock and never touched it!

Repairs were made, and we were on our way again, but not before word of our seemingly impossible quest to reach New York Harbor by July 4th had somehow made it to the NBC News Network. My brother Terry happened to be walking by the television sets at a Kmart in Adrian, Michigan, when he saw David Brinkley talking about the *Santa Maria*. Brinkley said, "The *Santa Maria* is struggling to get to New York.

… One man had an appendicitis attack, three more jumped ship, the cook, the engineer and the captain quit. They have no food, the bilge pumps are all burned out, it's taking on water, and it's SINKING!"

Terry shouted out, "Oh, no! That's my brother!"

The *St. Petersburg Times* called Barbara and asked her what she knew. She said, "I don't have all the information, but I know my husband. He'll make it to New York, if he has to get out and pull it!"

After the NBC News broadcast, it didn't take long for people to figure out where we were. They lined their cars up on the beach, with their headlights aimed at us. I needed to call home to ease Barb's worries, but in those days, there were no cell phones. We pulled the ship to a stop, and I lowered myself into the dinghy, fired up the engine, and started for shore. When I got close, someone yelled, "Here comes Columbus!"

I said, "I'm not Columbus; I'm Lowell Lytle, and I need to use a telephone!"

"Columbus needs to use a telephone!" They wouldn't let it die.

CHAPTER 24

BICENTENNIAL BREAKDOWN

Our warm southerly winds stayed with us for the rest of the journey. We sailed overnight to Sandy Hook, where all the ships were gathering to sail into New York Harbor, arriving early in the morning on Friday, July 2, 1976, with just the wind filling our sails, in an unbelievably thick fog. David Brinkley described the scene during the Nightly News, giving our beleaguered crew a nod:

A huge fleet of beautiful and entirely friendly ships is gathering outside New York Harbor, but the local officials are about as nervous as the British were in 1588 at the approach of the Spanish Armada—but for different reasons. The British were worried about a Spanish invasion and conquest; New York is worried about traffic jams, overcrowding, drownings and not enough bathrooms. The sailing ships are gathering around Sandy Hook today, to sail into New York grandly on Sunday.

There's talk of six or eight million people crowding in to see the ships, and the police talk of pickpockets crowding in to lift their wallets. There's $45,000 for extra portable bathrooms for the crowds, but not nearly enough. Towns in New Jersey advertise for the public to please stay away, that they couldn't handle them. The FAA worries about small aircraft overhead, colliding. Says one official, "We smell disaster." Well, whether or not all of that comes about, the ships are a beautiful site that no one is likely ever to see again.

And for those who have wondered, the Santa Maria, *the replica of Columbus' flagship, fighting its way up the coast*

with engine failures, crew problems and leaks ... the news is:
the Santa Maria did not sink. It is here and FLOATING!"[34]

By 7 a.m. Sunday morning, July 4th, the sun was up, but the fog was still so thick you couldn't see more than a few yards ahead. "Perhaps the fog would be thinner up in the crow's nest," I thought. Throughout the building and sailing of the *Santa Maria*, I had never been up in the crow's nest, basically a basket with a three-foot radius sixty feet up the main mast of the ship, intended to serve as a lookout perch. Now I climbed the ratlines to the top, but the fog was so thick, even at that height I could hardly see the main deck, sixty feet below. Suddenly, I heard a deep BOOOOoooooo and then heard a little screeching sound coming from our poop deck. It sounded like a cat being strangled.

Our first mate had a little reed instrument about ten inches long that he was using to warn other boats of our presence. If we were under sail, we were supposed to have the right of way—if we blew that little reed instrument. But all the while, I was still hearing "BOOOooooooooo!"

We were in the busiest harbor in the world, on the foggiest day possible, and he was blowing on that little dinky reed instrument. I shouted to the captain to use the automatic marine hailer. Every thirty seconds, it would make a loud noise for other boats to hear, but before they could start it up, I heard one of the crew members shouting, "BRACE YOURSELF FOR COLLISION!"

I looked down to the deck and saw the crewmen running about. Then I looked up about 30° higher than where I was sitting, and I saw a huge tanker coming right at me. I was sure it would cut us in half.

The captain yelled, "Starboard!"

The ship's boy was at the helm, and I believe he thought he was supposed to jump off the starboard side, because he now left the wheel and ran to the starboard side of the ship. The captain immediately ran down to the wheel and turned it hard to starboard. It was a brilliant move, forcing us broadside of that gigantic ship's wash. She slowly slipped by our spanker boom by no more than a foot and a half and, within seconds, disappeared into the fog. Shortly after this, we heard her anchor chain being dropped. Her captain probably thought, "There are some real crazy people out here today!"

Still in the crow's nest, I was shaking like a leaf, hanging on to a rope, while trying to get my size-thirteen feet into the ratlines, to no avail. I felt like a large clanger in a bell, as I hung there inside the crow's nest. When I finally made it down to the main deck, I said to the captain, "Let's get out of this area and see if we can find some eight-foot shoals to anchor, where these large ships can't hit us!" Anything shallower, and we'd scrape bottom. Anything deeper, and we'd be in the path of those great ships. We found a safe spot and stayed there for several hours.

Finally the fog lifted, but the wind started to blow, the seas began to build up, and our anchor didn't hold. We drifted right over some six-foot shoals and bounced six or seven times on that granite surface. BOOM! BOOM! BOOM! The ratlines shook, and the deck lowered one inch, and stayed that way. I looked at our deep-water sailors, and they looked like they were in shock. They were sure that the ship's back had been broken.

The ship's designer had told me to put an iron keel under the wooden keel, in case something like this happened. Then, he said, I wouldn't have to worry about it. He was right. After doing a complete inspection of the bilge, we found no leaks. There was some damage, however, to Mark Lach's psyche. He had been in the galley doing dishes when we went over the shoals, and because of the movement of the ship, he had gotten seasick and thrown up in the sink. Then, the moment we hit the shoals, Mark fell to his knees, and everything in the sink came out and fell on his head, along with all the dishes, pots, and pans from the cupboard.

We finally arrived under the Verrazano Bridge and headed into the bay, where we would sail past the Statue of Liberty, with five helicopters hovering over our heads taking pictures. Hours later, when we arrived at the dock, a newsman shoved a television camera in my face and said, "Mr. Lytle, if you had to do it all over again, would you do it?"

I shook my head and said, "Not without a maiden voyage to take care of all the insignificant things that could go wrong."

I watched the news that night. The editors cut everything from my response... except me shaking my head. I learned that day what a "sound bite" is all about.

As you can imagine, the next day was amazing. Doug Rosborough, the designer of the *Santa Maria*, was there to witness the event and later described the scene in his book from the spectator's perspective:

> *Through all the trials and tribulations, Lowell's indomitable spirit and faith succeeded, as his* Santa Maria *joined the host of other tall ships, big and small, and formed up for the grand parade of sail. Thousands of hearts beat as one as the* Santa Maria *and her crew of period Spanish soldiers and sailors in full dress, including a brown-robed priest perched on her high bow, holding his large crucifix aloft, led the flotilla of Class C ships under the Verrazano and up New York Harbor, past the Statue of Liberty and hordes of cheering spectators.*[20]

Seeing all those tall, square-rigged ships from around the world was something to behold. I think what I enjoyed most was watching Christopher Columbus, XVIII, standing on our poop deck in his dress whites, saluting the large Spanish training vessel as it passed. There was a ticker tape parade scheduled for the next day, to honor all of the crew members who had participated in the tall ships parade. Because of a long list of calamities, we arrived at the parade site in full costume but just after the honorees had passed, the street cleaners already cleaning up the mess. I grabbed an extra push broom from one of the workers and started sweeping the street. I figured I might get out of this with some dignity yet.

Wouldn't you know it? A nearby news crew was all over the image, and that night the evening news went nationwide with "Columbus Sweeps the New York Streets." Believe it or not, all of that news coverage gave us great exposure and helped in the months to come. The ship was very successful around the East Coast and the Gulf of Mexico for the next two years, sailing at night and on display during the day for thousands of elementary school children.

When I look back on the experience, it was fantastic. There is nothing quite like being at sea on a square-rigged ship with your belly full of food and the wind filling your sails. You cannot capture it with any form of media. It's something you simply must experience.

CAPTAIN'S LOG: THE SPIRIT OF CAPTAIN SMITH

Dateline: August 17, 2000 - ATLANTIC OCEAN
latitude 41° 43' 57" North, longitude 49° 56' 49" West

The bow of the *Titanic*... what an amazing sight! This was not a movie; this was the real thing. The Russian pilot took us right over the spot where Leonardo DiCaprio's character (Jack) held out his arms in the movie *Titanic* and declared, "I'M THE KING OF THE WORLD!" We went right over the main hatch, then slipped over the port side, to view the port anchor. It was so large we had to back away from it, just to get the full impact.

Swimming around the bow of the ship was an unusual sea creature. It was approximately five feet long, and its eyes were large, but it could not see. It was stark white and had a tail that looked like a rat, so naturally it was called a rattail fish. Our pilot called him Sam. There were some smaller ones he called "Sons of Sam." The pilot took the sub around to the crow's nest, which was now leaning against the bridge. I saw the telemotor, where the ship's wheel had been attached.

"I want to see the captain's cabin," I said. Minutes later, I was five feet from the captain's bathtub. We hovered in that spot, as they changed film in the camera, and I had time to imagine what the captain must have felt that night.

Then it was time to go to work. The pilot steered us back to the debris field. The first thing we picked up was a man's derby hat, perfectly preserved.

247

The lights of the MIR illuminate the deck of the Titanic[18]

The Titanic's telemotor as seen through the port hole of the MIR

To salvage debris, the pilot controlled two mechanical arms that acted just like a human hand. Whenever he picked an item up, he hit a switch that sent a basket out from beneath the sub, and then he released the object into the basket. When he released the man's derby hat, it didn't fall into the basket; it disintegrated like a cloud. At the time of our dive, it cost $4.87 per second each time the sub went down, and at that rate, we wanted to find something important. Can you imagine counting out five dollar bills every second for twelve hours?

I did spot something extremely important: the emergency telegraph that Officer Murdoch used to indicate Full stop, Full astern. It was a round mechanical device about two feet in diameter, with two handles on it that would move back and forth, and with an arrow pointing to various orders that would be transmitted from the bridge to a similar device in the engine room.

I also found a wrench approximately fourteen inches across at the mouth, sticking straight up in the ocean floor, as if someone had just thrown a javelin. Can you imagine the size of the nut that wrench had to turn?

I found a hot water heater, about four feet tall, with four Queen Anne legs made of brass, in very good condition. This water heater may have been in the dining room. Its purpose was to provide "instant" hot water so that tea could be served at any time. The technology on this water heater was amazing. You never want to boil fresh water at sea, for it just evaporates. This water heater would bring the water almost to a boil, and when you would put your cup under the faucet and turn it on, the heater would flash enough water to a boil just for that one cup. I found a rectangular first-class window, one of the items on our wish list. Everyone was glad to get it.

I tried to stay focused on artifacts and not get emotionally involved, but after a while, when you see a shoe or a hat, it just suddenly hits you. I felt like somebody had just kicked me in the stomach, and I had a fresh understanding as to what took place that fateful night. Fifteen hundred souls were on their way to New York to start a new life, and within two hours and forty minutes, they were gone.

As our submersible drifted past those places where Captain Smith would have been standing, making life and death decisions, where he would have surveyed the terrified passengers before him, their lives jeopardized because of the decisions of a few rich, powerful men, complacent in their trust of man's inventions, I began to feel the weight of his emotions, of his sorrow, the shock and pain, the tremendous sense of responsibility he must have felt.

As I continued to scan the debris field, looking at dishes, wine bottles, linoleum tile, and suitcases, I couldn't help but think how difficult it would be for me to say goodbye to my wife and children and put them on a lifeboat, knowing that I would never see them again. The last thirty minutes onboard that ship had to be horrible for those men. Lawrence Beasley, a second-class passenger on the *Titanic* who made it to a lifeboat, observed men standing on the deck in small groups praying.

Now, when I don that sharp uniform and get in character to play the role of Captain E.J. Smith, I remember that sensation, those emotions, and try to embody his spirit, as I walk among the visitors to the *Titanic* exhibit. I can sense their respect for the captain, but in real life, I am all too aware that I am not the one in control of my own life. I am very content to let God be my Captain, happy just to be a grommet on His ship. Without Him at the helm, I would have foundered countless times.

Finally, it was time for the sub to go back to the surface. I somehow hadn't noticed the freezing temperatures at the ocean floor. As we ascended to the surface, my legs began to cramp up in terrible pain, much like they had when I was in the bilge of the *Santa Maria* so many years before, trying desperately to keep the pump filter clear in similarly tight quarters.

The emergency telegraph found on Lowell's dive

I didn't think much about it at the time, but the crew of our *Santa Maria*, including my own son, had come so very close to facing a similar fate as we battled storms on our way to New York. Although we had all been terrified, we were all busy trying to save the ship and follow orders, trusting, hoping the captain knew how to pull us through, just as the crew must have done on the *Titanic*.

I was not the captain on the *Santa Maria*. Had I been, we surely would have perished!

DRY DOCK

In everyone's life, there are periods the Bible refers to as "the valley." In seaman's terms, this is known as "dry dock." Your ship is not even in the water, but set up on cleats upon the shore, her back to the sea.

Being in dry dock is hard to talk about. You wonder if this might be the end of your journey or just a test. If you are willing, your time in dry dock can truly be a period of repair, reflection and recuperation.

Marked often by great loss, every-day struggle, tremendous obstacles, the weight of past decisions, the downturn in life's circumstances, your time in dry dock could last months, years, or until the end of your days on earth.

In many ways, what you do while you are in dry dock may determine whether or not you will ever return to sea.

My trip to dry dock began subtly, through the hands of a thief.

CHAPTER 25

HENRY'S FINAL BOW

Although the *Santa Maria* project wasn't a direct part of our mission to deliver the Gospel, its success helped fund the Young American Showcase venture a little longer, and of course, there is always opportunity to share the Gospel—if you look for it.

Christopher Columbus had tried for seven years to get funding for his expedition, finally convincing Queen Isabella to support him by sharing with her the vision of being able to spread the Gospel to faraway lands. On our *Santa Maria* tours, elementary school children would walk through the ship, stopping at the forecastle, the hold and the poop deck, to listen to costumed sailors explain the history of the ship and its role in the "discovery" of America. When the children reached the Great Cabin, where Columbus himself would have stayed, a sailor dressed as a conquistador told them of the mission to spread the Gospel of Jesus Christ to all nations. The crew would hold their Bible studies in the Great Cabin as well.

The ship travelled throughout the main waterways of the country during the two years after the Bicentennial, giving tours for school children and appearing at special events, while Freedom Jam bands continued performing across the country, sharing the Gospel with millions of middle and high school youth in the night shows. On only one occasion, we managed to book the ship and the band at the same event. It was July 4th, 1978, when our "Freedom Jam" group was scheduled to perform at a huge Independence Day celebration in New Bedford, Massachusetts, giving several shows a day in an outdoor tent, while the *Santa Maria* was on display a few hundred yards away. Of course, I had to go.

Remember, Young American Showcase started in Florida with just one band, and I was a front man, singing, doing magic, and bringing out my dummy, Henry, to entertain the students in the day show. I had stepped out of performing many years before, as we expanded the number of groups and brought Lance Abair and other strong leaders in to train and manage the young men. Henry had been packed away carefully in a suitcase in my storage room.

Ventriloquism is a skill that takes a lot of practice and a lot of confidence. I now refused to perform with him, even though many of the band members asked me to. However, this event was special, and in a weak moment, I agreed to bring him out one more time. Barbara put Henry on a plane, and I picked him up at the airport (from the luggage carousel, of course). Before the band performed, we all gathered in the green room, which was a trailer just outside of the tent. Before long, someone banged on the door and said, "We're ready for you!" The guys ran out and into the tent and started their show, giving me time to get Henry out of the suitcase and run through my act.

Now, you need to know that it's very important as a ventriloquist that you treat your "vent figure," in this case Henry, as if he's a real person. The audience must be willing to believe, and if you go on stage with a dummy and fail to treat him as if he's alive, the audience will pick up on that, and the show will be embarrassing for everyone. Even during rehearsal, it's crucial that, when the dummy is sitting on your lap, you treat him as a living being. I got Henry out of the suitcase, put him on my lap, and started the routine. I said my lines, he said his lines, and that was it. After five years of inactivity, I had nothing. I couldn't think of what came next.

Of course, Henry, being a "real" person and a seasoned performer, was smart enough to know that there shouldn't be a gap between his line and mine, so he said to me, "Hey! There's a lot of dead air here."

"I know!" I responded. "I'm thinking!"

"Well, hurry up," he said, "we're on in five minutes."

"Just be quiet," I countered. "I'm trying to think of what comes next."

I know this sounds silly, and nothing like this had ever happened to me before. It was the first and last time. Someone once said, "If

My last time performing with Henry

a person talks to themselves, they might be going crazy, but if they answer themselves, they're completely nuts!" I wanted desperately for Henry to stop talking, so that I could gather my thoughts, but no—on and on he went.

I was starting to panic, all the old insecurities of my youth flooding back... when suddenly, there was a bang on the door: "You're on!" "Good grief!" I thought. "What do I do now?"

I quickly ran over to the tent with Henry, just in time to hear someone introducing me. In that moment, I was sure that I was about to face the biggest embarrassment of my life. I said a quick prayer, "God, help me remember." I ran to the microphone, put my foot on the rung of the chair, put Henry on my lap, and said my first line. He said his line, and the audience laughed! And that was it! With the laughter of the audience to bolster my confidence and my memory, the routine flowed.

That was the last time I ever performed with Henry. He was packed away in a storage building, along with many guitars and amplifiers. A short time later, the facility was broken into, and everything was stolen. Can you imagine what that thief thought when he opened the suitcase, expecting to find an instrument, only to see Henry looking up at him?

In my middle and high school years, having a vent figure helped me overcome my insecurities. Henry was with me that night in my bedroom after the *Horace Heidt Show*, when I gave him and my talents over to the Lord. Henry had done his part, playing an important role in my ministry and in getting Young American Showcase started. Now, he was gone.

I never got another vent figure. It just didn't seem right! As it turned out, 1978 would be a year of great loss.

CHAPTER 26

FIRE!

An oil painting of Lowell's replica of the Santa Maria *by Paul Garnett*

After New Bedford, the *Santa Maria* continued on her tour, north into Canada, then across the Great Lakes, finally making her way toward the Great Mississippi. Doug Rosborough's description of that route adds some detail to my own almost unbelievable story:

> *The Santa Maria continued on with her scheduled tour, hosted by hundreds of cities and towns in the United States and Canada, with over 500,000 visitors having gone aboard. Their ongoing guided tours, which included going below deck*

and then to Columbus' great cabin, offered a chance to relive the past and experience life afloat on a Spanish galleon in 1492. She continued with her many engagements for the next two years ... [once sailing] gallantly into Halifax Harbor, where I witnessed dozens of welcoming yachts and hundreds of spectators mark her reception as she docked at Privateer's Wharf for a three-day visit. She proceeded northeast and then down the St. Lawrence River to the Great Lakes, presenting herself en route. Next, it was down the Mississippi, destination: the Gulf of Mexico. [22]

Our plan was for the crew to eventually sail the *Santa Maria* back to St. Petersburg for regular maintenance and to give the men a much needed break.

Once they sailed out of the Great Lakes and began their journey down the Mississippi, along the way there would be two bridges north of St. Louis too low for the ship to pass beneath, so the main mast was removed and trucked around those spots to a town just north of Peoria, Illinois, while the ship travelled down river by engine power. While the mast was held in waiting for the *Santa Maria* to arrive, we arranged for a local carpenter to oil it down and rebuild the crow's nest.

When the ship arrived, they stepped the mast and started down the Mississippi to Peoria. On the way, the exhaust pipe from the generator came loose, filling the inside of the ship with black soot. That was one big mess to clean up. When that cleanup was accomplished, the crew sailed to Peoria, then on to St. Louis, where large groups of people came out to tour the ship.

Almost ten years earlier, in 1969, another replica of the *Santa Maria* had been built in Spain and was touring the U.S. waterways, spreading good will as she sailed. She docked in St. Louis by the Great Arch, exactly where we would dock a decade later. Some time during her fateful stay, a terrible fire broke out onboard, and she was destroyed, a vivid memory for the people of St. Louis. Had we known about this foreboding event, would we have changed our plans?

As our own *Santa Maria* stood moored at the foot of the Great Arch, I flew in to enjoy the sight and do a little media promotion from the ship. I finished a radio interview, spent some time with the crew, and then flew back home. All was well with the world. The program was a success!

After St. Louis, the next stop was to be Memphis, Tennessee. Five hundred schools were already booked there, and teachers were preparing history lessons to coincide with our visit. The ship left St. Louis and began traveling south toward Memphis on Saturday, November 4, expecting to reach Memphis the next day.

It was an unusually warm Sunday afternoon, and the captain decided to have the crew go aloft and tie on the sails. While the rest of the crew was up in the rigging, the cook was given the order to go below and start the Sunday meal. He went below and started up the generator, then headed to the galley. A few moments later, he smelled smoke. Had the exhaust come loose again? Assuming that the generator was at fault, he shut it down, closed the door, and returned to the galley.

Several minutes later, a strong smell of smoke was still in the air. The cook returned, only to find that smoke was coming from under the door in the aft cabin. As soon as he opened the door, fresh air rushed in to the thick black smoke-filled room, and immediately flames engulfed the area.

Slamming the door shut, he ran up on deck and called out: "FIRE! FIRE!" The crew came down off the rigging as fast as they could. One at a time, they each grabbed fire extinguishers and rushed below deck, holding their breath as they ran back toward the generator, and then aimed their fire extinguishers at the flames, trying to douse the fire.

Each time they did this, they were taking their lives into their own hands. They were desperate to save the ship, but they could not see and could not hold their breath long enough to get through the dangerous smoke. Fatefully, they decided to open the main hatch cover to release the smoke. Immediately, the oxygen-starved fire shot up the hatch and reached the main mast, just oiled a few weeks earlier.

When the mast ignited, the fire immediately shot all the way up to the very top. This caused a bit of panic, to say the least. The captain, now focused on saving the lives of his men and moving the burning ship out of the way of other boat traffic, drove it as close to the shore as he could, and then gave the order to abandon ship.

The crew released both of the lifeboats, only to find that one of them had not been tied down, so it was now drifting away. Crew members were grabbing their life vests and making preparations to jump overboard. They had just recruited a new crew member in St. Louis, and he had not been instructed on how to use a life vest. One of the other crew members tried to help him, as the fire grew around them, and he accidentally caught the life vest in one of the ratlines on the poop deck. The poor man was actually tied to the rigging. One of the crew later described him as looking like a dog being held over water, with his arms and legs flailing wildly, until he could free himself.

As tradition and duty demanded, the captain was the last one off the ship. He jumped from the poop deck through flames that were coming out from the port holes of the great cabin. There were diving tanks and lots of black powder on board, and no sooner had the captain hit the water, the ship exploded.

I was not onboard the ship that day. I was at home suffering my own tragedies, ironically, watching the Tampa Bay Buccaneers get pounded. I received a phone call from one of the crew members telling me about the fire. My heart sank. Thankfully, no one had been killed or seriously injured fighting the flames or escaping the ship. Losing the *Santa Maria* was devastating, both personally and financially, but what was done was done. There was nothing I could do about it. The next day, I flew up to see what remained of one of my dreams. Doug later wrote:

> On November 5, 1978, while under power, she caught fire and burned to the waterline. Fortunately, the crew were able to beach, and all ten abandoned without injury. Lowell told me later they had reinstalled the exhaust from a new generator and although the exact cause of the fire was never determined, it could have been due to the overheated generator exhaust. The next morning they returned to the scene, intent on salvaging cannon, rigging and engine shaft, etc. Scavengers had gotten there first, however, and her bones were picked clean.[23]

Smoke was still coming from the bow of the ship. The insurance adjuster came and met with the crew members, asking them one at a time what they saw. I was in the room, listening to each one explain how they ran down below deck with their fire extinguisher, discharging it in the direction of the generator, and what else they saw, heard, and experienced. From the time I received the phone call through the first few interviews that day, I was in denial, fixating on certain things on the boat, not yet grasping the larger picture, the greater loss.

After the sixth or seventh crewman told his story, my body started to shake. The shock was finally wearing off, and reality was setting in. Whether we understand it at the time or not, being able to keep calm in difficult circumstances and trust that God is in control is the hallmark of abundant life. God knows! This is what I have come to call "Faith Rest." Ultimately, it was Faith Rest that got Barb and me through that loss.

That brought us to the end of our story of the *Santa Maria*. All we had left were the photos, newspaper clippings, and memories.

Doug wrote:

All the crew who had served on her over the years had praise for her adventures and capabilities and were greatly saddened by her loss. Undaunted even by this reverse in fortune, Lowell maintained his faith, and when I last spoke with him, was planning a new project vessel.[24]

CHAPTER 27

THE LADY BARBARA

The *Santa Maria* was gone. However, there is something that gets into your blood after being on a square-rigged ship. I guess it's the salt air, or the wind filling your sails and pushing your ship through the waves. Maybe it's the sight and sound of it all. Whatever it is, Doug Rosborough was right; it got hold of me again and a few years after losing the *Santa Maria*, I began the process of building another galleon.

The *Santa Maria* had been a beautiful ship, but she was designed for practicality, not beauty. A seventeenth-century Dutch frigate, on the other hand, would be much more decorative and would allow me to do some creative sculpting work. In the seventh century, countries would adorn their vessels with a plethora of ornate sculptures. They would put their finest artists to work making these lavish-looking ships, just to impress other countries. After listening almost on a day-to-day basis to Doug Rosborough for two and a half years, explaining the building process of the *Santa Maria*, I felt that I would probably be knowledgeable enough to design my own ship.

I followed the lines of a Greek sponge boat, put on a forecastle and poop deck, placed the masts in the right location, and she turned out to be one of the best sailing ships all of her captains had ever sailed.

I found a German sculptor who lived in Chicago and had studied in Munich and got him to help create the ornamentation for the ship. He made a likeness of Barbara, and we put it on the bow as the masthead. I called the ship, the *Lady Barbara*.

She was a beauty, a swashbuckling, romantic tribute to the greatest wife a man could ever ask for, and she took us six and a half years to

Prepping a board, with the hull of The Lady Barbara forming behind me

build. Surrounded by friends and family, and with cameras rolling, my beautiful wife smiled lovingly as she stood at the bow of The *Lady Barbara* to christen her with a bottle of champagne, before her maiden voyage.

Underneath that brave smile, Barbara held hidden worries I was oblivious to until many years later.

We launched the ship in time to make it to New York and lead the Class C division of the tall ships for the Statue of Liberty's Centenary celebration on July 4, 1986, and we encountered very few problems. It turned out to be a very enjoyable trip... except for one time when I began to panic.

We were headed north about fifty miles east of South Carolina under full sail. We were gliding along smoothly when the wind began to freshen, and then it started blowing hard.

The Lady Barbara at the 1986 Statue of Liberty Centenary celebration

The ship heeled over, which scared the tar out of me, but at the same time, the ship darted through the water like a bullet. The true sailors onboard were thrilled with excitement, but not me!

I shouted to the captain and recommended that he take in some sails. The captain, who was at the helm at the time, turned around and looked at me with a big grin on his face. "Congratulations, Lowell," he said. "You've built a magnificent sailing machine!"

After the tall ships parade, I was contacted by a motion picture company out of Spain wanting to use the ship for a movie being filmed off the coast of Chiltepec, Mexico. We were supposed to arrive there shortly after Thanksgiving. This all sounded like fun, because it would be the first time one of my ships had gone to a foreign country. I wanted this trip to be a memorable experience, so I brought onboard a four-star chef, who was preparing food for four days before we even left. We had a Thanksgiving dinner like you would never believe off the coast of Cuba—turkey, pumpkin pie, and all the trimmings.

Our first stop in Mexico was at Isla Mujeres, "The Island of Women," where we decided to fuel up and freshen up before continuing our journey. We thought this would take a matter of hours, but we ended up staying there for three days, due to a cold front that the captain said was going to be coming through. A cold front, he said, meant heavy seas. I was more concerned about the money we would lose every day we delayed than the safety of the crew and ship. "This is an oceangoing vessel," I protested. "It should be able to take the high seas." The captain relented, and within a few hours, we were on our way. About six hours later, the front came through.

I wasn't standing watch at the time. In fact, I was lying on my queen-sized bed in the forecastle, dressed only in my undershorts, reading the book, *The Hunt for Red October*. I noticed that there was an increasing rocking motion, which didn't bother me at all. I loved being in the bow of the ship with that kind of action. It rocked me to sleep. But this was different. The bulkhead had two large portholes, eighteen inches in diameter, and two smaller eight-inch portholes, both open. I felt a little spray coming in from the two small portholes and figured that it must be raining, so I shut the portholes, turned on a fan, and went back to reading my book.

A few moments later, I heard a gurgling sound coming from the clothes hamper on the other side of the room. I looked down at the floor and saw three inches of water standing on the plush red carpet. I then glanced up at the two large portholes, and it looked as if I was looking into a washing machine. The entire bow of the ship was dipping under the water. I immediately got out of bed, opened the door to the main deck, and saw Ray Nicholas at the helm, with his yellow weather slick, fighting the driving rain, looking like a Gloucester sea captain.

I grabbed the hand pump that we used to get the fuel oil from the fifty-gallon drums into our fuel tanks and ran back to my stateroom. I threw the hose outside onto the deck, got on my knees, and started pumping. We had quite a ride that night, but we weathered the storm and landed in time to make the movie *Miss Caribe*. The ship then headed to St. Thomas, where we intended to use it as a tourist attraction, and I headed home. We had a fresh new crew, and spirits were high.

All of the crew members had new pirate costumes, along with a live scarlet macaw, and they were ready to entertain. I had nothing to worry about.

The Lady Barbara berthed in Snug Harbor

It was September 9, 1989, and a tropical wave began churning off the coast of Africa, working its way west and building strength as it crossed the Atlantic Ocean just north of the Equator. On September 11, it gained enough intensity to be given a name: Hugo. Then, on September 13, now just five days away from St. Thomas, Hugo was classified as a hurricane, quickly moving to a category-5 storm.

The captain asked some of the local sailors what preparations they should make for a situation like this. Their answer was to take the ship to Culebra, which is an island fifteen miles east of Puerto Rico. They said, "It's an island of safe refuge, with a protected bay, and no hurricane has ever gone over that island!" So the crew purchased extra anchors, along with some more rope, and headed for Culebra. When they arrived in Culebra, the bay seemed to be filled with boats. They put out their anchors and hunkered down for the worst. Hugo made a turn as well, ultimately passing directly over the island.

An oil painting of Lowell's replica of the Lady Barbara by Paul Garnett

The crew later told me it was horrifying. The captain said the hurricane came right over that bay and stopped, throwing pieces of boats in all directions. A husband and wife were in a yacht right next to The *Lady Barbara*, and they both perished, their mast falling and crushing the woman, while her husband was washed overboard and drowned.

The crew of The *Lady Barbara* hung on as long as they could, but after a while, the anchors refused to hold. Not wanting the ship to sink in the middle of the bay, the captain decided to drive it into the shallower waters of the shoreline. In the process, it plowed into other damaged boats and tore a hole in its keel. The ship was totaled, but no crew members were lost.

Hugo ultimately killed a hundred and seven people and caused billions of dollars in damage as it worked its way up the Eastern seaboard, the strongest hurricane to hit the Carolinas in more than a hundred years. Around Culebra, twelve people lost their lives to the storm. I thank God that all I lost was a ship.

A few days after the hurricane had passed, I sold The *Lady Barbara* to a man in Seattle. A few months later, he had completely restored the ship, and for the next four years, he sailed her through the Caribbean, down to Venezuela twice and back, living out his lifelong dream. She still sails, now called the *Jolly Roger*, repainted and fulfilling the childhood fantasies of someone else, somewhere in the Caribbean. The *Santa Maria* launched in 1976 and burned in 1978. The *Lady Barbara* launched in1986 and was crunched by Hugo in 1989. I was done with shipbuilding!

CHAPTER 28

REDEMPTION

Both ships did make good money while they were sailing, enough to help float other "ships," those rock n' roll groups sent out through Young American Showcase. But the ships had been expensive to build, and The *Lady Barbara* had not been in the water long enough to cover her costs. With the revenue from that ship now gone, the remaining groups on the road quickly began to drain our resources.

Long before, the effectiveness of the Young American Showcase ministry had started to wane. Live rock n' roll had strong appeal in towns where young people had little opportunity to attend concerts on a regular basis, but with the growth in popularity of MTV over the previous several years, this next generation of young people was more drawn to the captivating, but often rebellious, music video imagery they found at home through their television sets than the positive message we had to offer. We kept on as long as we could, selling off unnecessary inventory, doing our best to continue reaching students, not willing yet to let go of what had been such a powerful ministry, but in the end we held on too long. By 1991, we came to a painful end, filing bankruptcy and closing the doors to our property at Snug Harbor.

Barb and I were in our late fifties, with no resources other than our home, and no income. In many ways, I had lost my identity, my source of recognition and accomplishment that all human beings tend to hold on to. Our staff members, who had become family in every sense, faced the same loss. We had sixty-three employees at the time. It's hard enough to experience this kind of transition on your own, but to see loved ones who have invested so much of themselves into the ministry go through the same separation was worse in many ways.

We had to eat and had bills to pay. I was 59 and starting over. My resume read like a trip to Disney World: educated at a Bible and music college, built and ran two drive-ins, two ships, and one bankrupt ministry. Side interests included singing, acting, magic, ventriloquism, and sculpting. There was not much call for that combination of skills and experience. I did whatever I had to do, which often turned out to be pretty fun and interesting work. I would buy things at auctions, clean and fix them, then turn around and sell them. I drove a limousine for a while and had some pretty famous passengers: Donald O'Connor, Mickey Rooney, Van Johnson, Bob Denver, and others. I sang with a seven-piece vocal group for pay at yacht clubs and malls in the area. Barb and I worked for many seasons decorating cruise ships for Christmas.

My old friend Irwin "Shorty" Yeaworth brought me over to Aqaba, Jordan, on and off for five years to help him with a Disney-like project

Posing with a group of men working on The Jordan Experience in Aqaba, Jordan

he was developing called "The Jordan Experience." It was fascinating and difficult work, building authentic scenery for the exhibit.

None of the men I worked with knew English, so we communicated mostly through sign language. I performed some magic tricks, to show my friendship and earn their trust, and together we worked in 120° heat every day. I would "wash" my clothes at night by putting a couple of inches of water in the tub, adding some shampoo, and stomping on them while I took a shower.

Back in the states, I was always willing to do whatever it took to support my family. I once found a dumpster where a number of broken office chairs had been discarded. I pulled them out, repaired them, and set them alongside the road to sell to people driving by. It certainly was not a class act, but I was comfortable in knowing that God had provided income through this adventure. Perhaps God was trying to teach me humility. I sat there alongside the road, enjoying abundant life, selling someone else's trash, one chair at a time.

Although The *Lady Barbara* had been built in tribute to my loving and incredibly supportive wife, the finances surrounding her building and ultimate demise, as well as the loss of the ministry we had worked so hard to build for over twenty years, were harder on Barbara than I realized, harder than she allowed me to know, or than I was willing to recognize at the time. In fact, it wasn't until the writing of this book that she confessed to me openly how deeply stressful that time had been for her. She told me there were days when she would go to the grocery store, and just stand in the aisle and cry, and then go back home. She had always stood beside me, doing whatever had to be done to make our dreams happen, and now she continued to stand beside me, even as we returned once again to living lean.

While we were walking through those difficult years together, all of the young people who had journeyed with us in Young American Showcase and through our high seas adventures continued to grow and expand their own lives, finishing their educations, and then starting their own ministries or serving in some other way. Scattered all over the country, most found themselves in some sort of leadership position in their chosen professions. They became highly successful, with families of their own following in their footsteps, inspirational men and women of God of whom I am incredibly proud. I still hear from them regularly.

Many went on to become quite successful in entertainment or a related industry. That was the case with Mark Lach, our 15-year-old neighbor, who grew up with our children and then worked on the *Santa Maria*—helping build her and then working the galley as she sailed. He eventually found himself working as Vice-President and Creative Director for RMS *Titanic*, and as that exhibit was being developed in Orlando, and the owners tried and failed to find an actor suitable to play the role of Captain E.J. Smith, and he called me.

You may recall from Chapter One that, after more than three hundred and fifty actors had been auditioned to no avail, Mark realized that he knew someone who would fit the bill, his very own former boss and neighbor from across the street. And I was hired. So, now we have come full circle in this almost unbelievable story.

I hope that my sharing briefly about those lean years gives some understanding about how God works, and perhaps strengthens the ability of the reader to find their own Faith Rest. So many of us walk through those times where we feel we have been hauled out of the ocean and put up on dry dock, and we are unable to sail forward in our lives, much less sail out into the deep.

This is true for many, as it was true for Barb and me as we approached our senior years. It can feel as if our lives have peaked and are waning, as if our purpose is being fulfilled by younger and younger people, as if our value in the world's eyes is dropping. But in God's eyes, our value never wanes, and our mission never ends—as long as we are still breathing. It may be time to find a new path, a renewed passion, but part of Faith Rest is understanding that "it's not over" and that God has a plan.

CAPTAIN'S LOG: STROKE, STROKE!

Dateline: June 2012 - ST. PETERSBURG, FLORIDA

April of 2012 marked the one-hundred-year anniversary of the sinking of the *Titanic,* and that kept me pretty busy. Pigeon Forge held a memorial event, with fifteen descendants of those who had been on the *Titanic,* including Molly Brown's great-granddaughter and descendants of Isador and Ida Straus and 2nd Officer Charles Lightoller. It was an amazing experience attended by thousands of visitors.

That same month, Barbara and I were invited to take a *Titanic* Memorial Cruise that would cross over the spot of the sinking on the anniversary. I was to give four lectures during the trip and hold a memorial service once we reached the particular spot where the ship had gone down. The cruise ship travelled from Puerto Rico to New York, then up to Halifax, Nova Scotia, where more than a hundred and fifty victims were buried.

There I saw the tombstone of John Hume, one of the brave musicians who played to calm the passengers as the ship sank. We headed out from Halifax toward Dublin, Ireland, and stopped right over the site of the sinking, the same site I had been to a few years earlier to take the dive down to the wreckage. About a hundred people threw flowers into the ocean at the conclusion of the service.

Roger Bansemer was able to go back to that site for a second dive in 2005, five years after our first trip together, becoming the first artist to actually paint a portrait of the *Titanic* at the site of the wreckage, twelve thousand, five hundred feet below. The day after his second dive, before the *Akademik* left the area, he made arrangements for a unique experience. Boarding one of the Zodiac rubber craft and wearing only his street clothes, Roger donned a life vest and slipped off the edge of the watercraft into the chilly water, making these sobering observations as he tried to adjust to the temperature:

We're right over the bow of the Titanic; it's 12,500 feet below us straight down. I'm not kidding, it really takes your breath away; this is cold. [It was 50°F and the water was about 28°F when the Titanic sank.] I didn't think it would be this cold. I'm just imagining being out here at night, when all you can see is the stars and maybe a little bit of the moonlit ocean. I was up on the bridge last night looking, and I couldn't see the horizon, just total darkness. The Titanic would be heading for the bottom right now. You would have been on a lovely ship when you hit the iceberg, then two hours later, you would have been in the water, just like I am now. It's a pretty incredible thought.[25]

When asked why he decided to have this experience, he said:

Back in 2000, when I went down on my dive, I didn't think about everybody on the surface. This space right here is just as much a part of history as the bottom is, because this is where most of the people, where their lives ended.[26]

The day after the memorial service on the *Titanic* Memorial Cruise, the sea was very rough, with high winds. Seawater splashed way up on our windows. The crew of the ship said it hadn't been that rough for seven years. The following day, the captain got on the horn and said they'd just run into an ice floe, five miles wide, with icebergs. The ice floe had drifted farther east than normal. You can believe the passengers on that ship were more than a little concerned, wondering if they had tempted fate too far. Thankfully, we had learned something from the *Titanic* experience and didn't try to plow through the ice floe.

Harper Memorial Baptist Church

Instead, we went south, and as a result, missed time for a shore excursion once we reached Dublin. At our next stop in Glasgow, Scotland, Barbara and I went to John Harper's first church, Paisley Road Baptist Church (now renamed Harper Memorial Baptist), then down to Southampton before flying back home.

After a very busy spring, I had a little time off, keeping busy taking care of things around the yard and house, spending time with Barbara and our children and grandchildren. In late June, I had some cancerous spots removed from my face, not unusual when you live in Florida. The doctor said not to bend over and to stay in bed and rest. I did... for three whole days, but that was about my limit. I went out one morning to do some lawn work, but three hours later I was out of wind and had to lie down—unusual for me. Later that afternoon, my grandson wanted me to go swimming with him. I got my suit on, but then as I stepped in the water, I got dizzy. I sat down, but then fell backward.

The next thing I knew, he was pouring water on my face, and Barbara was calling the doctor, who urged her to bring me to the hospital right away. To give you an idea of how stubborn I am, unaccustomed to serious illness even at age 80, I insisted on stopping at the cleaners to pick up some pants on the way to the hospital. After test results were back, the doctor came in and said, "I've got some bad news. You have a massive blood clot on your lungs." Then he added, "Most people who come in with this are already dead." I might have died at the cleaners.

When they discovered the blood clot on my lungs, they took me off of baby aspirin and put me on a blood thinner. Doctors don't like to mix aspirin with any blood thinners because it's quite a dangerous mix. If I were to fall or have an accident, I could bleed to death. They told me that within eight months to a year the blood clot would dissolve, and it did. However, I had to continue to take the blood thinners, to prevent future blood clots.

Then, just ten days later, I suddenly had double vision, and a stinging sensation ran down my right arm and leg. I called to Barb, my speech slurring badly. I was having a stroke.

They did a more thorough checkup this time and found that the two arteries in my neck are unusually small—I was born that way!

The blood thinner was reaching the larger blood vessels, but not the smaller ones. They immediately took me off of it and gave me a heavy dose of aspirin. After one week, they started me on the blood thinner again.

As doctors were working to reduce the damage from the stroke, calls were going out to family and friends, and within the hour, word was spread through phone and the magic of the Internet, and people all over the country were praying for me. After all those years, those young musicians and boat crew, now grown with families and careers, some of them grandparents themselves, remembered an old man who once had a crazy vision for sharing the Gospel, a man who put them through some of the hardest years of their lives to fulfill that vision, and they began to pray and also to tell more people, and more, and more.

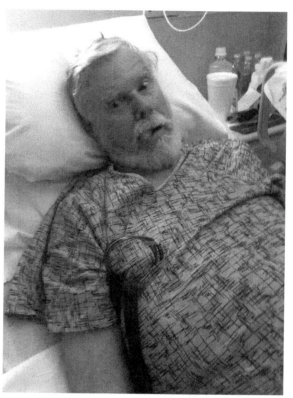

Clowning around in the hospital after my stroke

My *Titanic* family was praying, too, worried about my health and knowing better than anyone that this could be the end of my career portraying the captain. They also knew how much that role had meant to me and what a godsend it had been to my family.

The stroke had taken my vision. My right arm and leg were useless, so I could neither walk, nor write. My face was characteristically drooped on one side, and I spoke with a slur. Yes, this was a time when I had no choice but to rest in my faith, completely helpless and dependent upon God to guard my family and my future. I had to trust that, whatever might come, He knew what was best. There was nothing left to do but have a little fun with it.

Just one week later my vision came back, and after about a month, I was able to walk (although still badly out of balance), and the sag in my face gradually disappeared. Three weeks in rehab helped improve my walking, the use of my arm, my balance and speech. Though I can grip and hold things with my right hand, I am unable to write or sign my name. I cannot type, but I can speak, and I'm grateful for that.

That first week in the hospital, I had no idea if I would be able to return to my role as the captain. Miraculously, I was able to resume the work, more quickly than anyone had hoped.

For the first several months, I felt extreme and rather constant pain in my ears. No one around me could have known just how excruciating it was. One evening, after a day's work at the Pigeon Forge *Titanic* exhibit, I decided to drive, just to distract myself from this horrible pain. Pigeon Forge sits in a picturesque valley at the gateway to the Great Smokey Mountains, just a few miles from Gatlinburg in one of the most beautiful parts of the country. I found a side road that headed straight up the mountain and took it as high as I could go. Then, as I sat at the top, enjoying the glorious view, I suddenly realized that the pain in my ears had subsided. I stayed there a long time, wondering if the pain would return when I went back down the mountain. It didn't! I would be comfortable through the night and for several hours the next day, and then the pain would return. Driving up those mountain roads became a nightly ritual, and after several months, the pain gradually faded away completely.

I know I've still got the potential at any moment for another clot to form and break loose and either cause another stroke or send me straight to Heaven. Like many people who have had a stroke, I'm on a lot of medications to keep my blood thinned, so even the slightest fall could easily cause me to bleed to death. The truth is that any number of things could kill any of us at any moment. Death is inevitable, and as we age we are more aware that our time to leave this earth is approaching. We have to make a decision: will we stay home, avoiding even the slightest risk and spending our nights worrying about what might happen? Or, will we make the most of the life we've been given, trusting that God has an appointed day and time for each of us to meet Him face to face?

How about you? Are you able to enjoy what I call "Faith Rest?" If you have faith in God, if you truly believe in and know Him for who He is and believe that He has everything under control, then you can leave your fears and worries behind and keep getting up every day and doing whatever it is He wants you to do.

DRY DOCK

CHAPTER 29

FAITH REST

There were many times over each of our adventures together when Barbara stood, not just as my helpmate, but also as my partner, working hard to support each ministry, caring for our children, and stepping into leadership when she was needed. No matter what adventure I was on, her presence would always call me home again and keep me centered on what was important. Home meant family, comfort, rest, and restocking for the next adventure. Home meant safety and security in an atmosphere of unconditional love, a perfect picture of Heaven.

Over the years, Barbara, too, had to learn Faith Rest, sometimes, regrettably, because of my decisions, most often because it is a skill we all need in life, whether we take great risks or no risks at all. I had watched Barbara endure constant pain and countless hospitalizations and surgeries over our more than fifty years together. She'd had so many operations and lived with an awful lot of pain, always handling it with grace and peace. That is Faith Rest.

Through those times when my life had been in jeopardy, Barbara definitely had to rely on Faith Rest. She told me the time she most feared was when I took the submersible down to the site of the wreck of the *Titanic*. As noted earlier, I was the oldest person to make the dive, and before I could go we had to have all of our affairs in order and sign a waiver, because the conditions there could change rapidly. I made it back, of course, and life went on as normal... until my stroke revealed the condition I now live with daily.

Barbara, though, was getting more and more frail. Around 2010 she was diagnosed with both osteo– and rheumatoid arthritis and began taking medications for those ailments. Then, in January 2012, while we were returning home from Pigeon Forge, we both got the swine flu. Weakened by the flu and having difficulty moving because of her painful arthritic condition, Barb took a bad fall, in which she broke her arm and dislocated her shoulder.

Barb's arm needed pins to set her broken bones and a sling to keep her shoulder and arm immobilized. After she was released from the hospital, our daughter Laura met us in Georgia and drove us back to Florida. Barb was a beautiful pianist and had continued to play regularly even through her arthritic pain, but this most recent injury left her unable to continue playing. This was a true disappointment for her that she gently accepted, resting in her own faith that everything was happening in its time.

Over the next several months, Barb continued to suffer. We struggled through what everyone fights today with the medical system: difficulty sharing records among multiple doctors and hospitals, no one monitoring overall care, and overlapping and sometimes dangerous drug combinations. She fell eight times and lost 75 lbs. that year. Finally, her doctor took her off of all medications, to give her body a chance to stabilize, and she began to do much better.

In the Spring of 2013, our grandson was being honored for achieving the rank of Eagle Scout at a ceremony in Huntsville, Alabama, a significant event we all wanted to attend. Barb was feeling so much better and was in her element. She loved setting a decorative table and spent lots of time in the kitchen preparing food for the occasion. She seemed to be doing great. Then, when we got home, she came down with bronchitis, spending night after sleepless night with coughing fits.

Not wanting to keep me awake, Barb went to the front room to sleep. Even in our eighties, we still loved to cuddle; every once in a while during the night, I would pat her arm, and she knew that meant "I love you." I always heard "I love you, too." I don't know if I slept any better, not having her next to me to cuddle that night, but she slept better and the next night went back out to the couch.

Sometime after midnight, Barb got up to put the cat in another room, and in the darkness she tripped over a chair and fell, hearing a cracking sound as she landed. She called and called for help, but none of us heard her... until about 1 a.m.

I called 911 and the ambulance took Barb to the hospital. Her body was shaking, she was in so much pain. They had to do X-rays, draw blood, and did not give her anything for the pain for the next three to four hours. X-rays showed that she had severely fractured her hip.

After she was admitted and settled in her room and was resting comfortably, the staff told me to go on home. It was about 5 a.m. Five hours later, I awoke and went back to the hospital to see her. She was lying on her back, and I could see that her breathing was labored, but I didn't think anything of it. "She's in the hospital, so they should know what's going on," I thought to myself.

About fifteen minutes later, a group of doctors came through and asked questions about her condition (instead of reading her chart). They tried to wake her up, but she would not rouse. She kept snoring, and now she seemed to me to be gasping for air. "We'll come back in about an hour," they said. "Apparently, she's tired." And the whole group turned and left.

I stayed for about ten minutes more before getting up to walk down the hall. I was about a hundred feet away when I heard over the loudspeaker that doctors were being called to an emergency in room 301. That was Barb's room. I quickly returned to find four doctors at her bedside, and within a few moments, there were fourteen doctors and nurses.

Because of my height, I could see what they were doing. They gave her something to counteract the narcotics she had received earlier, but they still could not get her to wake up.

Then I heard a gurgling sound. They were trying to suction out her lungs, but had trouble getting the tube down her. When they were finally successful, her eyes opened just for a moment. I could see mucous and blood coming out of her lungs.

Barb's breathing was better, but she was still unconscious. All but one of the doctors left. "I'll be back," he said. "I'll be watching her all the time. She's on blood thinners. We need to operate but can't until the blood thinners work out of her system."

Over the next several hours, Barb began to wake up, but with her hip broken right in two, she was in extreme pain. I would reach over and pat her arm, like I did every night at home, and she would smile. She knew I was there loving her.

I went home around 7 p.m. that evening, exhausted. About 1 a.m. I received a call from the hospital. Barb had taken a turn for the worse and had been moved to the ICU. I immediately let our children know and then rushed back to her side.

The doctor on call said that Barb was in dire condition. "She's had three heart attacks," she said. "We resuscitated her three times, and she's on a respirator now. We're pumping things into her to stabilize her blood pressure."

I was confused. Why had they said just hours before, "She'll be all right; we just can't get her awake," and now, just a few hours later, that she was in critical condition? They were trying to work on her, but, I knew in my heart that she was already gone.

If you've ever witnessed someone being resuscitated, you know that it is a violent procedure, painful for the patient. The ICU nurse later told me, "You might not want to resuscitate her again because she's probably not going to recover, but we'll wait until the morning and ask the doctor who comes on." With the help of the life-support system, Barb continued to breathe through the night, as we waited for the doctor. He came at about 7 o'clock the next morning, and after examining Barb's progress, he turned to me and said, "I'm sorry to say that her kidneys are failing, and her liver is failing."

"Is she dead?" I spoke to him abruptly, needing to hear a clear answer from him in the midst of my confusion and exhaustion.

"Yes," he replied.

I was heartbroken. So many people have faced this devastating moment, but until you do, you cannot imagine what it feels like. After reconciling myself with the truth of the matter, I authorized them to turn off the machines that were keeping her alive. I kissed her on the forehead, and then started bawling like a baby.

Barb's ICU nurse was a Christian. She put her arms around me in that moment, and we prayed together. My children were waiting anxiously down the hall in a sitting area, my grandchildren asleep in chairs beside them. I left Barb's side to tell them that their mother and grandmother was gone from this life.

Barb died early in the morning on June 10, 2013. Since then, there have been so many Christians praying for me and giving me strength, and I've felt it. The support has been wonderful, from family and friends, from Showcase members and from my *Titanic* family. Prayer changes things. It really does.

For years, I had been active, doing so many different things, and had not had a lot of time alone to myself. Now, I would be going home without Barb. Thank God the house would be full of kids and grandkids, with remembrances of Barbara all around us. You could never ever find a more loving woman.

A beautiful thing happened two weeks before Barb passed away. She and I were lying in bed together, reminiscing about all the things we'd experienced over the years, all the things we'd done and seen together, far more than I could ever include in this book. We laughed and had a good time thinking about it all. We'd never really done that before. I guess we were too busy making new memories.

Death is a part of life, and for all of us, there is a time when we will be separated from our loved ones. Part of my Faith Rest is that I know beyond a shadow of a doubt that Barb is no longer in pain, is whole and completely well for the first time in decades, and is enjoying her next exciting adventure to the fullest.

God is sovereign. He knows when our time is due. Still, I wish I could have had ten more years with her.

CHAPTER 30

FULL CIRCLE

Looking back, my latest adventure with the *Titanic* came about as a result of careful orchestration, not by me, but by God. It's so amazing to see the many times He has brought me full circle, has shown me that everything in my life, circumstances and choices both good and bad, had His hand on it. That insecure boy who found his identity through a last-minute ten-cent purchase grew to be a man who would use his skills honed in vacation Bible school to show many people how to rest on the lap of God, under His loving control.

That little kid who fought for his brother's love and respect would see their relationship grow, be broken and restored again, as, all the while, still more people would be shown God's restoring grace. The creative energy of a young teen building a fighter plane in his family's barn was channeled into building drive-ins, ships, companies, and lives. Along the way, countless people heard the restoring message of Christ.

A young man's brazen method for finding love through a paper heart became the key to finding the love of his life, and through that couple the message of the unfailing love of God continues to be shared. Now, separated in death, they have the great hope of coming home together again, full circle, on the other side of this incredible journey. A small child finding his voice at the feet of his mother threaded all the way through to a *Titanic* adventure, and as a result, still more lives are affected by hearing the voice of yet another man committed to saving souls, the voice of Rev. John Harper, not silenced by his death in 1912, but given a chance to speak again more than one hundred years later.

CAPTAIN'S LOG: Final Entry

Portraying Captain E.J. Smith

You've now read many stories about my life and about how God works. Yes, He does work in many mysterious ways. You can see that over the past eighty-plus years I've had an uproarious misadventure, dramatic twists and turns, one natural disaster after another, incredible explorations, danger on the high seas, personal foibles, deep losses, and multiple crises of faith.

Any or all of this could take a person away from a belief in a loving God. That I haven't lost my faith is not a testimony to my faithfulness to God; it is a testimony to His faithfulness to me and to His own Word. Romans 8:28 tells us that "all things work together for good to those who love God and are called according to His purpose." He has never failed to show His workings through me, even in the worst of times. And He has always honored His Word by giving me a peace that surpasses all human understanding.

Still, in all of the circumstances of my life, grief of the magnitude I felt in losing my beloved wife had never before been one of my experiences. Now, I keep the wonderful memories of our love, shared over the space of fifty-eight years, deep within my own heart and alive through my children and grandchildren. That God has further plans for me is obvious, because I am still standing up and breathing in.

It may have become cliché to say that God loves you and has a wonderful plan for your life, but this is exactly how it has worked out for me, and I would be wrong to not recommend it. You and I may be at different stages in our human lives, but from the standpoint of eternity, we are all standing with one foot in the grave. We are all treading icy waters, heading for a long darkness. As I leave you, I will play the role of Rev. Harper, swimming among the survivors in the water, asking each in turn, "Have you accepted Jesus Christ as your personal Savior?"

Whatever He has for me in the days ahead is a new story. I look forward with an open mind and humble heart in eager anticipation for the title of yet another chapter of *Diving into the Deep*.

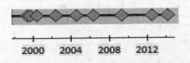

TITANIC ADVENTURE

When I was 80, adventure called again. I was no longer surprised to hear from him; he had been nagging me about this particular journey for many years.

This time, I finally said "yes," and the result is in your hands. Now, I can't wait to hear from him again.

Thank you for taking this journey with me, and please remember my story the next time adventure calls you!

D. L. Moody's Illinois Street church, destroyed in the 1871 Chicago fire [30]

Stereoscope image of the Chicago fire aftermath

BONUS STORY:
THE GREAT CHICAGO FIRE

[This fascinating and sometimes hilarious true story was not included in the original printing of "Diving into the Deep", but gives us a glimpse of a different way of life as well as a convicting insight and important message for us all. The story picks up after Lowell's big decision from Chapter 6 but stands on its own as part of Lowell's greatest hope for his readers. Enjoy!]

Though the Great Depression was all but over by the beginning of World War II, its devastating effects on families continued for decades. As I graduated from high school and prepared to study at Moody Bible Institute just five years after the end of World War II, my father was still struggling to make ends meet. If I wanted to attend Moody, I would have to find my own way to cover the cost of tuition and living expenses.

Someone told me they were hiring salesmen for a unique project on Wabash Avenue in downtown Chicago, about a one-mile walk from Moody Bible Institute. I heard about an upcoming meeting and decided to go down one Monday morning and see what it was all about. When I got to 203 North Wabash Avenue, I saw a large building several stories tall, with an illuminated sign in the shape of a vacuum cleaner on the roof that could be seen from several blocks away. This entire section of Chicago was burned to the ground eighty years earlier in the Great Chicago Fire of 1871, the same fire that destroyed D. L. Moody's first church in Chicago, as well as his home and the homes of most of his parishioners. Moody himself gives credit to this fire for helping him solidify God's call on his life to preach the Word of God to the world. Dr. Stephen Flick of Christian Heritage Fellowship recounts what happened that fateful night to have such an impact on this world-renowned evangelist in his essay, "D. L. Moody's Lost Opportunity" [32]:

On Sunday night, October 8, 1871, the well-known evangelist, D. L. Moody, preached to the largest congregation that he had yet addressed in Chicago. His text that evening was, "What shall I do then with Jesus which is called Christ?" (taken from Matthew chapter 27 verse 22.), and at the conclusion of his sermon, he said, "I wish you would take this text home with you and turn it over in your minds during the week, and next Sabbath we will come to Calvary and the Cross, and we will decide what to do with Jesus of Nazareth." Then his song evangelist Ira D. Sankey, whose hymns are sprinkled throughout most evangelical hymnbooks, began to lead in singing the hymn

Today the Savior calls; for refuge fly;
The storm of justice falls, and death is nigh. [33]

But Sankey never finished the hymn, for while he was singing the rush and roar of fire engines whistled by the church on the street outside, and before morning much of the city of Chicago lay in ashes. To his dying day, Mr. Moody deeply regretted that he had told that congregation to come next Sabbath and decide what to do with Jesus. "I have never since dared," he said, "to give an audience a week to think of their salvation. If they were lost they might rise up in judgment against me. I have never seen that congregation since. I will never meet those people until I meet them in another world. But I want to tell you of one lesson that I learned that night which I have never forgotten, and that is, when I preach, to press Christ upon the people then and there and try to bring them to a decision on the spot. I would rather have that right hand cut off than to give an audience a week now to decide what to do with Jesus."

As I walked up to the ornate art deco structure on Wabash almost eight decades after that terrible night, I had no thoughts in my head of fires, of D. L. Moody, or the urgency of the Gospel as far as I can remember, but an ember of truth started smoldering in my heart that morning that continues to burn today.

Stereoscope image of the Chicago fire aftermath

This building still stands and can be visited today, renovated in 2014 to house a boutique hotel. Around 1953, Dearborn Bank moved in and remained for decades, but in 1950, this address on North Wabash Avenue was headquarters to Health-Mor, the manufacturer and direct sales operation for the Filter Queen, a high-end bagless vacuum still sold today in almost the same form as the original model. I was a little tardy as I opened the thick brass front door and entered the tall atrium lobby, but as I stood there, I could hear many men's voices echoing off of the marble walls and floor.

I noticed a stairway leading to the second floor where the voices were coming from, so I headed up. When I arrived at the top of the stairs, I saw a large open area with at least one hundred men milling around and talking with one another, all in nice suits and ties, some with images of vacuum cleaners on them. Lined up along the wall were dozens of Filter Queen vacuums with their cardboard accessory boxes. Boy, were those men loud, but they all seem to enjoy each other's fellowship!

A few minutes later, a man I later learned was the sales manager stepped up to something that looked like a pulpit and said, "Everyone take your seats." I looked around and saw approximately one hundred fifty banged up metal chairs, each with a little song sheet placed on the seat. There was a piano up on the platform, and as everyone quickly found a chair, the sales manager enthusiastically said, "Turn to Number Three in your song sheets!" The man on the piano played a rousing introduction, and all those smiling men started singing to the music of an old college fight song:

"Oh when those Filter Queen salesmen fall in line,
They never fail to show their products fine.
They get the name up on the dotted line.
The only words they know are SIGN AND SIGN AND SIGN
And so we FIGHT, FIGHT,FIGHT for every sale!
To pass the order book, we'll NEVER FAIL,
And if they don't sign quick we'll
stick and stick until their licked!
Filter Queen, LET'S GO!"

Filter Queen Model 350 [31]

I could hardly believe it. One hundred grinning men dressed in snappy suits and ties singing a corny song about a vacuum cleaner! When they got through, the manager said, "Who's got a testimonial?" Immediately, ten men jumped to their feet. They would start by telling some of the things that they had done the week before to convince a customer, usually a housewife, that she needed to buy this "cleaning system." One by one, they would tell their stories and then sit down. When seven or eight of them got through, the manager said, "The rest of you, sit down," then gave us a stirring pep talk:

"DON'T YOU DARE GO OUT AND TRY TO SELL A VACUUM CLEANER!" he shouted. "They already have one! You sell HEALTH!!"

"Eighty percent of the most infectious diseases come from the germs we breathe, not the ones we eat or drink. Germs can't run, skip, fly, or float! They ride on something, and that's dust! When you're in that home, you need to show them dust and dirt! Use the Filter Queen in front of their couch. Turn off the machine and dump it on their carpet in front of them. Let them see the dust and the dirt! If the man is in the house, tell him about the motor. It has two propelling fans, six inches in diameter; a Black & Decker type motor. It works with centrifugal force. It has a lifetime service guarantee! Now GO GET 'EM!"

I was in awe!!

One hundred men picked up their machines and ran down the stairs and knocked on virtually every house in the city of Chicago in one year's time; just one hundred motivated men reached practically the entire Chicago population of over 3.6 million people!

Week after week, I would attend Bible classes and sell vacuums whenever I wasn't in class. Every Sunday morning, I would go to the Moody Church, sit in a pew and sing songs, listen to some testimonies, and listen to the preacher give a talk. At Moody, even when people were invited to the front to receive Jesus Christ as their personal Savior, most were already believers, or thought they were. Like every other church I know of, never once did a single member of the congregation, much less the whole crowd, ever jump up enthusiastically and run out the door to share the plan of salvation with anyone, not even at Moody!

By contrast, every Monday morning I would sit in that vacuum cleaner sales meeting. Not ever did we invite a customer to come to us, listen to us sing our songs, give our testimonies, and finish with the sales manager giving a rousing speech before asking if they would like to step forward and buy a vacuum. They didn't leave it to the sales manager! They went out into the field themselves! They were doing it right!

The New Testament church was a place where Christians could meet and fellowship together, sing songs, and study the word of God, and then they would go out to where the people were to share the Good News. When did that change?

In my years of ministry, at times I would go out on the street corner with a microphone and a tape recorder to do street interviews. I would stop and ask people, "Can you tell me how to get to heaven"? I would hear things like "Be good to your fellow man," "Don't kill anybody," "Go to church at least twice a week," "Live the Golden Rule." One man said in all sincerity, "I think it's about fifteen miles from Orlando." What a shame.

As Christians, we are all ambassadors for Christ. We are either good ones or bad ones, but we all represent our God. Suppose you were born over two thousand years ago in Jerusalem, and imagine you witnessed Christ's death, burial, and resurrection. Would you be shouting it from the rooftops? Let's just say Christ's resurrection happened today and you knew it to be true. What would you do differently than you do right now to tell that story? Wouldn't you run to everyone you saw and tell them that wonderful news? If that's the case, then why should two thousand years and six thousand miles make any difference?

I've been told that 97% of all Christians have never led a soul to Christ. As for me, I want the whole world to know who Jesus Christ is, why he came, and what they should do about it! I trust you do, too!

Sharing your faith isn't hard, but it does take an ounce of courage and sometimes a little creativity. Just like sharing my faith, selling vacuum cleaners required me to learn creative ways to get through when doors were, sometimes literally, slammed in my face. I was a poor college student with no car, so the sales manager would carry those of us with no transportation to various parts of the city and drop us off. After several hours, he would come back and pick us up.

Just like today, in 1950, Chicago had a large population of immigrant families, most from Ireland, Poland, and Germany. After World War II, a flood of new immigrants came to Chicago, and these families moved to neighborhoods and parishes where one could live their entire lives and never have to speak a word of English. One Saturday morning, I was dropped off in one of the many Polish districts. I found myself in front of a two-story apartment house, two apartments on the bottom floor and two on the top. I knocked on the first door and gave my customary introduction.

Queen for a Day *Promo photo from WABC Radio*

In the early 50s, most home entertainment was centered around the radio, and Health-Mor sponsored a very popular radio show called *Queen for a Day* with host Jack Bailey. Housewives all across the country would listen every week and dream of being crowned and receiving all those prizes.

I would begin, "Hello, my name is Lowell Lytle. Have you ever heard of the radio program *Queen for a Day*?" They almost always said, "Yes!" "Well," I would continue, "my company helps sponsor that program. As you will recall, many gifts are given to the contestants, and we have a gift for you today! Here is your hand-painted boudoir basket." It was nothing more than a waste basket from the local Five and Dime that the company provided for us.

Typically, the "lady of the house" is now holding the basket in her hand and feeling a little bit obligated to cooperate with whatever I said next, which was always, "I have another item to show you that we give away on that radio program." Then, I would normally go behind the bushes, pick up the vacuum cleaner, walk through the door, and make my presentation.

Well, it didn't work that way on the first apartment. After I said my lines, she said, "No speaka da English." I apologized and moved on to the next apartment. I banged on the door, the lady opened it, and again, I said, "How do you do? My name is Lowell Lytle. Have you ever heard of the radio program *Queen for a Day* with Jack Bailey?" She replied, "No speaka da English." I apologized and marched upstairs with my Filter Queen, all the time thinking, "This is just GREAT! They've dropped me off in a spot where no one speaks English! How in the world am I going to make any money today?"

I'm on the second floor now, and I knocked on another apartment door hoping that someone could speak my language. The lady came to the door, I said my usual routine, and of course, she said, "No speaka da English."

I excused myself and proceeded to the last apartment, thinking all along, "Something's wrong with this picture. How can people live in Chicago and not know how to speak

English?" I had to sell vacuums to pay for college, so failure wasn't an option. I kept thinking, "It doesn't make sense. I think they're on to me! I think they know I'm trying to sell them something!" My brother had taught me how to speak what we called "double talk," similar to what some folks call "Pig Latin." I tried to do something that would bring out the real truth.

I went to the very last door and knocked. When the lady came to the door. I said, "Ki-ban yi-bou si-beak di-bubble ti-balk?" She wrinkled her brow and said to me, "Can't you speak English?" I said, "Sure can lady, here's your wastebasket!" After that, she listened to my opening, let me in, and I walked through the door and gave my presentation.

I didn't make the sale. Ni-bice tri-by! (Nice try.)

By now, you know that God blessed my work as a Filter Queen salesman, even giving me extra sales one day so that Barb and I could finally set a date to be married. He also used the lessons learned in those years to fan those embers into flame and give me the vision to move far beyond the walls of the church to reach people right where they are. In this bonus story, I want to encourage you to examine your own commitment to sharing the plan of Salvation without delay or excuse. Start praying for opportunities to share your faith today and then learn these following Scripture verses in any version you wish (this is the New International):

Romans 3:23 *"...for all have sinned and fall short of the glory of God..."*

Romans 6:23 *"For the wages of sin is death, but the gift of God is eternal life in Christ Jesus our Lord."*

John 1:12 *"Yet to all who received him, to those who believed in his name, he gave the right to become children of God-"*

John 3:16 *"For God so loved the world that he gave his one and only Son, that whoever believes in him shall not perish but have eternal life."*

Why? Because faith comes by hearing, and hearing by the Word of God! (Romans 10:17) Never underestimate the power of God's Holy Scripture to work in people's hearts.

I remember when I was selling, it was always in my mind to "close the deal"; in other words, ask for the sale! It's the same in sharing your faith. Don't just keep rambling on; ask the question. Don't be afraid to say, "Would you like to receive Christ in your heart right now?" Our fear of asking this question keeps so many from taking that step.

When I'm leading someone to Christ, I give them an opportunity right then and there to receive Christ. Learn from D. L. Moody's example! Timing is everything; life can be short. You may not have another opportunity with this person; "Today is the day of salvation!" (II Corinthians 6:2)

You may want to share your own testimony, because no one can dispute personal experience. Start by sharing your testimony with someone you trust and ask them to share theirs. Recall the details: How old were you? Who led you to Christ, and where were you? What was your life like before, and how did it change you? If you cannot remember anything about your own testimony, there is a chance that you may not know the Lord as your personal Savior. You may know a lot ABOUT Him, but not know Him personally! You may have attended church your entire life but never actually asked Him to be your Lord and Savior! Don't be afraid; it could be that your eyes were not opened by God to understand until this very moment!

I've got good news! Today can be the day you can be sure, the day the great Chicago fire begins in earnest inside of you! I've written a simple prayer of Salvation following this story, but you can also just pray to Him in your own words.

Dear Lord,

I believe that You died on the cross and rose from the dead for my sins. I ask You to come in to my heart to save me from my sins and be the Lord and Master of my life.Help me to live for You. Thank You Lord, for saving my soul!

In Jesus name I pray.........Amen!

Did you just pray that prayer? Welcome to the family! I would love to hear from you, and my contact information is included in the next few pages.

ENCOURAGE
PUBLISHING

AUTHOR CONTACT

You may contact the author in any of the following ways:

Email: lowelllytle@gmail.com
Phone: (727)460-3178
Mail: Lowell Lytle c/o Encourage Publishing
1116 Creekview Circle, New Albany, IN 47150
Internet: www.*Titanic*Talk.com

Diving into the Deep is also available in hardback, as an audiobook for purchase or digital download, and as an e-book.

Individual downloads are available through Amazon's Kindle and Audible, iTunes, and other licensed distributors.

Individual copies of the print and audiobook versions may be ordered direct from the publisher, at Titanic Museum in Pigeon Forge and Branson and from your favorite bookseller or wholesale distributor. Resellers can find this title in the Ingram/Spring Arbor catalog or may call the publisher directly.

For additional comments, permissions, to inquire about book signing and speaking events, or about special discounts for resellers and multiple copy purchase, contact the publisher:

Encourage Publishing
812.987.6148
info@encouragebooks.com
www.encouragebooks.com

TO LEARN MORE

To hear Lowell tell about Rev. John Harper and other stories, visit:
www.*Titanic*talk.com

To see videos of Lowell and his brother building the drive-in or Lowell performing magic and ventriloquism, search for "Lowell Lytle" at www.youtube.com.

To keep track of Leslie Turner's projects, visit:
www.encouragebooks.com

To follow Roger Bansemer's artwork, visit:
www.bansemer.com

To follow Gary Horton's ministry, visit:
www.youthontrack.org

Or create your own Titanic experience at:
www.Titanicpigeonforge.com
www.Titanicbranson.com or
www.rmsTitanic.net

REFERENCES

1. Photo courtesy of G. Michael Harris
2. Ibid.
3. Text by Julia H. Johnston, music by Daniel B. Towner
4. Photo by Jill McClane Baker
5. From a poem by the same name written by C.T. Studd
6. Photo of original Abbott's, used by permission
7. Photo courtesy of G. Michael Harris
8. Photo credit: Cedar Bay Entertainment
9. Bansemer, Roger, *Journey to Titanic* (Sarasota, FL, Pineapple Press: 2003)
10. Photo courtesy of G. Michael Harris
11. Ibid.
12. Ibid.
13. Ibid.
14. Rosborough, Doug, *Confessions of a Boat Builder* (Dobbs Ferry, NY, Sheridan House, Inc.: 2001)
15. Photo credit: Tony Lopez
16. Bansemer
17. Photo courtesy of G. Michael Harris
18. Ibid.
19. Ibid.
20. Rosborough
21. Photo courtesy of G. Michael Harris
22. Rosborough
23. Ibid.
24. Ibid.
25. Bansemer
26. Ibid.
27. Photo courtesy of G. Michael Harris
28. Ibid.
29. Ibid.
30. Courtesy of The Moody Church
31. Courtesy of www.vacuummuseum.com
32. Courtesy of Dr. Stephen Flick, Christian Heritage Fellowship
33. "Today the Saviour Calls" by Samuel F. Smith and Lowell Mason
34. Courtesy of Vanderbilt TV News Archive, 110 21st Ave. S, Suite 704, Nashville, TN 37203

RECOMMENDED READING

The following references were used in the research of this book and are all interesting and recommended reading:

4 Steps to Peace With God. Billy Graham Association: peacewithgod. jesus.net

Caffery, B. (1976, May 13). "Sea Captain: Pipe Him Aboard, Mate." *The Evening Independent.*

Confessions of a Boat Builder. James Douglas Rosborough (Dobbs Ferry, NY, Sheridan House Inc.: 2001)

God's Forever Family: The Jesus People Movement in America. Larry Eskridge (Oxford, Oxford University Press: 2013)

How to Play Madison Square Garden. Mindi Abair, Lance Abair and Ross Cooper (2013)

Journey to Titanic. Roger Bansemer (Sarasota, FL, Pineapple Press: 2003)

The Sinking of the Titanic. Abridged and edited by Bruce M. Caplan (Seattle, WA, Miracle Press: 1997)

The Titanic's Last Hero. Moody Adams with Lee W. Meredith (San Jose, CA, Rocklin Press: 2012)

Just Finished Reading?

The author would love to hear from you. Send your responses or questions directly to Lowell at lowelllytle@gmail.com, or through the publisher.

Please post your thoughts and reviews online at Amazon.com, goodreads.com, shop.encouragebooks.com, barnesandnoble.com, or other online literary rating sites. Your honest review is important to us, is strongly encouraged and deeply appreciated.

Order Additional Copies

Diving into the Deep is available as paperback, hardback, audiobook in physical and download format, and ebook, through the usual online channels, through your favorite bookstore or at:

www.encouragebooks.com

Resellers, libraries, non-profits and those wishing to order multiple copies may order through the usual channels or contact Encourage Publishing directly for additional discount.

Library of Congress Control Number: 2017933578

Cataloguing data:
Lowell Lytle, Leslie Turner
Diving into the Deep: A Gripping True Story of Adventure,
Risk, and Spiritual Quest

ISBN 97809962067-5-4 (paperback ed.)
ISBN 97809962067-4-7 (hardback ed.)
ISBN 97809962067-3-0 (audiobook ed.)

ENCOURAGE
PUBLISHING

A WORD FROM THE PUBLISHER

Encourage Publishing is honored to serve as publisher and distributor for "Diving into the Deep". In fact, we know that our very existence can be attributed to the hand of God bringing us together with Lowell and the lessons we've learned from his inspiring life stories.

For this we are indebted to Lowell. We enjoy the privilege of helping others bring their stories to life, expressing sometimes extremely difficult and always important messages in a captivating manner, true to their style and voice. We LOVE OUR AUTHORS and would be happy to speak with you about your project.

Encourage Publishing
812.987.6148
info@encouragebooks.com
www.encouragebooks.com